EDITOR:

 MEN-AT-A

THE AUSTRIAN ARMY 1740-80: 2 INFANTRY

Text by
PHILIP HAYTHORNTHWAITE
Colour plates by
BILL YOUNGHUSBAND

First published in Great Britain in 1994
by Osprey, an imprint of
Reed Consumer Books Ltd.
Michelin House, 81 Fulham Road,
London SW3 6RB
and Auckland, Melbourne, Singapore and
Toronto

ISBN 1 85532 418 0

Filmset in Great Britain by Keyspools Ltd
Printed through Bookbuilders Ltd, Hong Kong

Artist's note

Readers may care to note that the original paintings
from which the colour plates in this book were pre-
pared are available for private sale. All reproduction
copyright whatsoever is retained by the publisher. All
enquiries should be addressed to:

Bill Younghusband
12 St Mathews Walk
Chapel Allerton
Leeds
LS7 3DS

The publishers regret that they can enter into no
correspondence upon this matter.

Publisher's note

Readers may wish to study this title in conjunction
with the following Osprey publications:

MAA 236 *Frederick the Great's Army (1) Cavalry*
MAA 240 *Frederick the Great's Army (2) Infantry*
MAA 248 *Frederick the Great's Army (3) Specialist
        Troops*
MAA 271 *The Austrian Army 1740–80 (1) Cavalry*

For a catalogue of all books published by Osprey Military
please write to:

**The Marketing Manager,
Consumer Catalogue Department,
Osprey Publishing Ltd,
Michelin House, 81 Fulham Road,
London SW3 6RB**

THE EMPIRE AND ITS INFANTRY

The composition of the Habsburg Empire and its military forces is summarized in the first part of this study, *The Austrian Army 1740–1780 (1): Cavalry* (MAA 271). The present volume concerns the bulk part of the army, the infantry.

At the accession of Maria Theresa in 1740 the Austro-Hungarian army included 52 infantry regiments, of which three were Hungarian, three Netherlandish and one Italian. The remainder drew their recruits not only from the Habsburg territories, including Bohemia, Moravia and Silesia (the last being lost to Prussia in 1742), but from the autonomous states of the Holy Roman Empire and beyond. When regimental numbers were assigned perma-nently in 1769, there were 57 regular regiments, including 11 Hungarian, five Netherlandish and two Italian. Prior to that date one regiment each had been disbanded from the Netherlands, Lombardy, and Switzerland. There were in addition the *Grenz* or border infantry regiments (to be covered in Part 3 of this study).

A significant change which occurred during this period was the increase in the proportion of regiments raised in Hungary, the government of that state (of which Maria Theresa was queen) having from 1741 made their contribution more in keeping with the comparative sizes of the various Habsburg territories. Although the Hungarian regiments were part of an integrated military system, Hungary remained a separate kingdom, part of the empire only by reason of the Habsburg possession of the crown of Hungary; for this reason all non-Hungarian units were commonly styled 'German', irrespective of their actual place of origin.

'Foreign' personnel, including many officers,

Grenadiers, c. 1748; a painting, presumably from life, by David Morier. Left: Regt. Los Rios (no. 9): white uniform with green facings and waistcoat, buff breeches, yellow buttons; cap with green bag, yellow or gold lace and tassel. Centre: Regt. Waldeck (no. 35): white uniform with scarlet facings (but white lapels and turnbacks), yellow buttons, cap with brass plate with yellow or gold lace and tassel. Right: Regt. Wurmbrand (no. 50): white with scarlet facings, white buttons, red cap bag with white or silver lace, brass badge on waist pouch. Only the central figure has a red stock, the others black; note the facing-coloured collars, the varied arrangement of buttons and different patterns of belt, and the narrow strap for the waist pouch of Regt. Wurmbrand. (The Royal Collection © Her Majesty the Queen)

Grenadiers, c. 1748; a painting by David Morier, which includes Regt. Ujváryi (no. 2), right, wearing characteristic Hungarian costume: white coat with yellow pointed cuffs, turnbacks and lace, blue waistcoat and breeches with yellow braid and buttons, yellow sash with blue barrels, brass cap grenade, blue cap bag with yellow or gold lace and tassel. Note that the bayonet and sabre appear to have separate, dark brown belts. The other grenadiers have scarlet cuffs, and the central figure a scarlet collar; yellow buttons, and red cap bags with yellow or gold lace. The cap at left has a red plate bearing a brass grenade and scrolls, and white metal edge; this man has a scarlet stock, and a sabre with a scarlet 'cravat' between hilt and scabbard throat. The central grenadier has a black stock and a sabre with small shell-guard; note the arrangement of his coat buttons, one over two over three. (The Royal Collection © Her Majesty the Queen)

comprised an important part of the military establishment. However, many of the Germans from areas outside the Habsburg possessions were less 'foreign' in language and outlook than genuine Habsburg subjects from regions like Hungary or Italy, and the definition of what constituted a foreigner is further complicated by the fact that many who bore foreign names were not themselves new emigrants from their native states. An example is provided by three of the Austrian army's most distinguished Irish field-marshals, all of whose families left Ireland after the Battle of the Boyne. Maximilian Ulysses von Browne (1705–57) was born in Basle, the son of Ulysses von Browne (d. 1731), himself a distinguished soldier of the Habsburg army and a count of the empire from 1716; Maximilian's uncle Georg von Browne (1698–1792) became a field-marshal in the Russian army. Franz Moritz Lacy (1725–1801) was born in St

Petersburg, the son of an exile of 1690 who had a distinguished career in the Russian army. Carl Claudius O'Donnell (1715–71), count of Tyrconnell, also came from an Irish emigrant family and was a kinsman of the Spanish field-marshal Henry Joseph O'Donnell (1769–1834).

Although the nature of some members of the Austrian army was not as 'foreign' as their names might suggest, it is interesting to note that of the *Inhabers* (colonel-proprietors) of infantry regiments during the period 1740–1780, almost half had non-German names, and the proportion of 'foreigners' to Austrians is even greater when the Germans originating from outside the Habsburg lands are considered. (More than twenty *Inhabers* bore Hungarian names, a similar number had names suggesting a French or Netherlands origin, 13 had Italian names, nine Irish and three Scottish).

Recruiting

Recruiting was conducted primarily by the regiments, involving both voluntary enlistment and conscription. Volunteers were attracted by cash bounties, with infantry sometimes offered only half the amount the cavalrymen received, the mounted regiments thus having the pick of recruits. Many recruits came from outside the Habsburg domains; even during the brief period when the imperial crown passed from the hands of the Habsburg family to those of Charles Albert of Bavaria (Emperor Charles VII), thus depriving the Austrian recruiters of access to much of the empire, the recruits from non-Habsburg territories still represented almost one-fifth of the total. Official recruiting-grounds within the empire were not assigned to regiments until 1766, but before that date many maintained a 'national'

Grenadiers, c. 1748; a painting by David Morier. The left-hand figure, to which an identity of Regt. Browne (no. 36) has been ascribed, has green facings, white buttons, no lapels, red stock, and upon the waist pouch a white metal coat of arms and separate grenades at the sides. The cap has a green plate with white metal border and brass grenade, and a green bag with white or silver lace. The right-hand figure has scarlet facings, yellow buttons and pouch-grenade, black stock, and a scarlet cap bag with yellow or gold lace. (The Royal Collection © Her Majesty the Queen)

Grenadiers, c. 1748; a painting by David Morier. This depiction of unidentified regiments includes a significant side view of the grenadier cap (note also the great length of queue). The left hand figure has bright blue facings and breeches, blue cap bag with yellow or gold lace, yellow buttons and red stock; the grenadier at right has scarlet collar and cuffs, no lapels, white turnbacks, black stock, and red cap bag with yellow or gold lace. Note how clearly the white stockings show with coloured breeches (left), and the same figure also appears to show the use of reinforced or leather gaiter-tops. (The Royal Collection © Her Majesty the Queen)

identity by drawing recruits from a particular area. Not until September 1756 were the Netherlandish and Italian regiments permitted to accept recruits from any part of the empire, and only from January 1758 were Hungarian regiments allowed to enrol foreigners and deserters of any nationality.

Enlistment was initially for life, but to encourage a superior grade of recruit limited service was introduced from May 1757, by which men could enlist for only six years or the duration of hostilities; eventually up to one-third of all recruits enlisted under these terms. Voluntary enlistment was supplemented by a limited form of conscription, but this applied only to the Austrian and Bohemian lands, and produced only limited numbers of recruits who were not always of the best quality. A wider conscription was devised at the end of Maria Theresa's reign, by which men were trained for two years and then permitted to return home for all but six weeks' annual training; but this system never extended to Italy or the Netherlands and only later to Hungary and the Tyrol, coming into

effect in 1781. The traditional method of forming Hungarian units was by a feudal levy or 'Insurrection', but the regiments raised for the army were organized on the same system as those from the 'German' parts of the empire.

The officer corps was not so much the aristocratic élite as it was in some armies, it being possible for an officer of humble origin to rise by his own merits; but an officer with aristocratic connections, or wealth, could achieve accelerated promotion. Although there was no official system of purchase of rank, the empire's council of war (*Hofkriegsrath*) demanded a payment for each promotion, although candidates for higher rank had to have been deemed worthy in the first place. Family influence was an undoubted advantage. For example, the distinguished field-marshal Leopold Daun (1705–66) had been intended for the church, but with a father and grandfather who were both general officers it was probably inevitable that he should make his career in his father's regiment. He served with it in Sicily in 1718, and duly rose to command it. (This regiment, numbered 56 in 1767, was finally named after him in 1888).

There was no prejudice against foreign officers, even those who came to Austrian service from another army: the career of Ernst Gideon Loudon (1717–90) being one of the most distinguished examples. Born in Livonia of a Scottish family who had settled there in the 14th century, he served first in the Russian army before applying to Frederick the Great for a Prussian commission. This was refused (it was said because Frederick remarked, 'The physiognomy of this man does not please me'!), so instead Loudon joined Trenck's Pandours in the Austrian army. If the story is true, it is interesting to reflect upon the consequences of Frederick's dislike of Loudon's face, for in later campaigns he became one of the Prussian king's sternest opponents.

An incident in Loudon's career demonstrates the leadership expected of Austrian officers. At the siege of Belgrade in 1789 he assembled his staff at the first parallel and informed them that they must not retreat one step: 'Here is the spot where we must either conquer or die . . . I shall exert my utmost efforts to attain the proposed end, but I also desire that every one do his duty. I wish every one to prepare for victory or death, and to consider that none of us were born not to die.'

REGIMENTAL ORGANIZATION

Each regiment was headed by its *Inhaber* or 'colonel-proprietor', who enjoyed almost complete control over the regiment's finances, training, recruiting, and over the appointment and promotion of its officers (not until 1765 did the *Hofkriegsrath* assume the appointing of field officers). Although the rights and influence of the *Inhaber* declined during the period under review, and although actual command of the regiment was vested in the colonel who led it, the *Inhaber* remained much more than merely a titular colonel-in-chief, and even gave the regiment his name. As a result of the use of the *Inhaber*'s name by

Grenadiers, c. 1748; a painting by David Morier, including Regt. Salm-Salm (no. 14), right, with black facings and white buttons. This is an example of a cap bag not in the facing colour: scarlet, with white or silver lace. The others have blue facings, left with yellow buttons and blue cap bag with yellow or gold lace; centre, yellow buttons, blue bag with white or silver lace, and cap plate blue with brass grenade and white metal edge. (The Royal Collection © Her Majesty the Queen)

his regiment, to prevent confusion to the reader, throughout this book regiments are identified by numbers in parentheses, these being the numbers assigned permanently in 1769; to clarify unit lineage they appear in this text even for dates preceding the allocation of numbers.

Some regiments kept the same name for many years. At the beginning of Maria Theresa's reign nine infantry regiments had borne the same name for over 20 years (nos. 7, 18, 20, 23, 24, 28, 45, 47 and 56), of which the oldest name was that of Regt. P. Daun (no. 56), whose *Inhaber* had been in place since 1690. During the period under review six regiments had an *Inhaber* of 50 years' standing (nos. 7, 9, 23, 45, 47 and 56), the longest-serving being Joseph Harrach of no. 47, *Inhaber* for some 60 years (1704–64). Regt.

Stahremberg (no. 24) kept the same name even longer, from 1703 until 1771, although this involved two successive *Inhabers* with the title of Graf Stahremberg. Conversely, regiments might have many changes of *Inhaber* and title; during the reign of Maria Theresa, for example, Regts. 22, 41, 46, and 49 each had five *Inhabers*, no. 22 having five within a period of 17 years.

Confusion can arise from two regiments bearing the same name at a different time; for example, Regt. Harrach was the title borne by no. 47 from 1704 to 1764, but by no. 7 after 1774. When two *Inhabers* bore the same surname at the same time their regiments might be distinguished by the use of their first name (e.g., Regt. Nikolaus Esterházy, no. 33, and Regt. Josef Esterházy, no. 37); or by giving the

Grenadiers, c. 1748; a painting by David Morier, showing Regts. Lothringen (no. 1) and Arberg (no. 55). The Lothringen grenadier, left, Σxing his bayonet, has scarlet facings, waistcoat and turnbacks, yellow buttons, scarlet cap bag with yellow or gold lace, and a brass coat of arms on his waist pouch; note the white gaiters, shown here uniquely among the Morier paintings. Regt. Arberg, right, has scarlet facings, waistcoat and breeches, yellow buttons, and a cap with a red plate bearing a brass grenade and edge. Note how the white stockings show clearly against the red breeches. (The Royal Collection © Her Majesty the Queen)

regiment of the senior *Inhaber* the prefix 'Alt' and that of the junior 'Jung' – hence 'Jung-Wolfenbüttel' (no. 10) and 'Alt-Wolfenbüttel' (no. 29), both *Inhabers* being members of that state's ruling family.

Considerable differences in the spelling of names may be encountered in contemporary sources, especially non-German names, e.g. Ujváryi or Ujvary, Kökemesdy or Kökenyesdy, Lacy or Lascy, etc.; but similar variations may be found even in the case of German names, e.g. Baden or Baaden, Deutschmeister or Teutschmeister. In some cases spellings changed during the period; the family name of Gideon Loudon was often spelled 'Laudon' or 'Laudohn' by German-speakers, the latter being used by his family, until in 1759 he reverted to the original Scottish 'Loudon'.

Throughout the period rank structure remained reasonably constant. Below the *Inhaber* was the colonel-commandant or *Obrist* (a contemporary spelling of the modern *Oberst*; the *Inhaber* was sometimes styled *Obrist-Inhaber*). The other field ranks were those of *Obristlieutenant* or lieutenant-colonel (similarly, 'lieutenant' was used in place of the more modern *leutnant*), and *Obristwachtmeister*, re-named *Major* from about 1757. Other officers were the company captain (*Hauptmann* or *Hauptleute*), with his subalterns the *Lieutenant* and *Fähnrich* (or *Fandriche*, an ensign). In 1759 the rank of *Fähnrich* (*Cornet* in the cavalry) was replaced by *Unter-lieutenant*, with *Lieutenants* being styled *Ober-lieutenants*. As field officers nominally retained command of a company, the new rank of *Capitän-lieutenant* was introduced in 1748 for the officers who actually commanded field officers' companies. Below the commissioned officers were cadets of various grades, serving with regiments in preparation for receiving a commission; the senior of these were styled *Fähnen-Cadeten*. From 1752 only two-thirds of new officers entered by this route: the remaining vacancies were reserved for graduates of the military academy at Wiener Neustadt.

The senior NCO rank was that of company sergeant-major or *Feldwäbel* (*Feldwebel* is the more familiar modern spelling). Below him was the *Führer*, who frequently carried the colours, and the company clerk or *Fourier*, together responsible for the company accounts and muster rolls. These three ranks were known as the *Prima Plana*, from their names

Recruiting the army: an NCO attempts to persuade a civilian to enlist. (Print after R. von Ottenfeld)

appearing originally on the first page of the muster roll. Beneath them were the *Corporals*, each responsible for one of the company's *Corporalschaften* or platoons, and the lance-corporals or *Gefreiters*; also part of each company, though not of NCO rank, was the *Feldscher* or medical orderly, and usually two batmen (*Fourierschützen*). The number of officers and NCOs in each company was less than those provided in some other armies, at a cost in efficiency to the Austrian regiments.

Although regimental organization remained reasonably standard, establishments and strengths varied considerably, apart from the usual diminution in strength as a result of the rigours of campaign. At the beginning of the reign of Maria Theresa regiments consisted of three battalions, each of five fusilier companies, plus two grenadier companies. The establishment of a regiment at this date included one *Obrist*, one *Obristlieutenant*, one *Obristwachtmeister*, 17 *Hauptleute*, 17 *Lieutenants*, 17 *Fähnrichs*, 17 *Feldwäbels*, 15 *Führers*, 16 *Feldschers*, 83 *Corporals*, 34 *Fourierschützen*, 150 *Gefreiters*, 49 drummers, 172 grenadiers and 1,396 fusiliers. In addition, the regimental staff included the quartermaster (*Regiments-*

quartiermeister, an officer of lieutenant's rank), the *Auditor* (legal officer), the chaplain, the adjutant (*Wachtmeister-lieutenant*, a senior NCO), the surgeon (*Regiments-Feldscher*) and the provost (*Profoss*), usually a retired NCO. Added to these were the officer cadets, an armourer (*Büchsenmeister*), and in wartime a *Wagenmeister*, an NCO appointed to organize regimental transport.

A number of organizational changes occurred during the period. In 1748 an additional company was added to each regiment, and the organization altered to four battalions of four companies each (five companies in Hungarian regiments), plus two grenadier companies; in the same year the number of *Fähnrichs* was reduced to eight per regiment. From 1752 the surgeon was redesignated as the *Regiments-Chirurg*, a title perhaps implying a higher level of skill than did *Feldscher*. From 1756 each regiment comprised one garrison and three field battalions of four companies each, plus two grenadier companies, reorganized in wartime into two field battalions of six companies each, a garrison battalion of four companies, and the two grenadier companies. As a result of the increasing tactical significance of the battalion, to ensure a sufficiency of field officers an extra major

Above: 'German' infantry: fusilier drummer, left, fusilier, centre, and grenadier, right. Note that but for the drum belt and laced wings the drummer's uniform is identical to that of the fusilier. (Print after R. von Ottenfeld)

German infantry: company officer, left, field officer, centre, wearing boots for mounted service, and grenadier, right. (Print after R. von Ottenfeld)

was added to each regiment during the Seven Years' War, although the appointment was only made permanent in 1769.

It became increasingly common to detach the grenadiers from their regiments and to concentrate them into élite grenadier battalions, initially upon an *ad hoc* basis. This not only formed units of (theoretically) the regiments' most stalwart men, but was a way of increasing the number of tactical elements within a small force. For instance, by the formation of two grenadier battalions each seven companies strong, the small Austrian infantry contingent with the Allied army in Flanders in 1744 was increased from six to eight battalions. In 1769 the practice was regularized by the formation of 19 permanent élite battalions, 14 of three 'divisions' (i.e. six companies) each and five of four 'divisions' each (i.e. four companies). Five of these were deployed in Bohemia, three each in Hungary and Moravia, two each in Lower Austria, the Austrian Netherlands and Styria/Carinthia, and one each in Upper Austria and Transylvania. Two further battalions were created in 1770. The component companies continued to wear the uniform of their parent regiments.

A constant schedule of numbering infantry regiments was introduced in August 1769; and a new establishment was instituted in the same year, a regiment consisting of two field battalions of six companies each, one garrison battalion of four companies (expanded to six in wartime), and two grenadier companies. At this date a grenadier company comprised one *Hauptmann*, one *Oberlieutenant*, one *Unterlieutenant*, one *Feldwäbel*, four *Corporals*, one batman, two drummers, two fifers, one pioneer and 99 grenadiers. Fusilier companies were similar but for one *Führer*, eight *Gefreiters*, one fifer and 91 privates. Regimental staff included the *Obrist* (sometimes styled *Obrist-Regimentscommandanten*), *Obristlieutenant*, one (later two) *Major*, chaplain, *Auditor*, *Rechnungsführer*, two *Fähnen-Cadetten*, adjutant, regimental surgeon, battalion surgeon and eight assistants, nine *Fouriers*, one provost and one drum major. (Despite the statistics quoted above, actual company-strength during the period is stated to have been about 130-160 of all ranks).

The garrison battalion, composed of the less fit men, was intended in part to provide a reservoir of reinforcements for the regiment's two field battalions; but during the early Seven Years' War it was found necessary to employ them in the field, and in 1757–58 a depot was established for each regiment to supply reinforcements. Traditionally, the first company of the first battalion was that commanded by the *Inhaber* and was termed the *Leib-Compagnie* (a relic of the practice of a commander maintaining a personal 'lifeguard'). From 1769 the practice was extended when the regiment's battalions took the titles of *Leib-Bataillon*, *Obristens-Bataillon*, and

'German' infantry fusilier wearing full equipment; note the suspension of the bayonet scabbard in a frog from the waist belt. The regiment depicted is one of those which used scalloped lace on the hat. (Print after R. von Ottenfeld)

Obristlieutenants-Bataillon, the latter previously styled the *Garnisons-Bataillon* (garrison battalion).

Not all regiments were organized as above. For example, when Salomon Sprecher von Bernegg raised the regiment which bore his name in 1743 from the Tyrol and Voralberg it comprised two grenadier and 20 fusilier companies, about 2,600 men in all. Conversely, when the *Tiroler Land- und Feld-Regiment* (no. 46) was accorded the status of a line regiment in 1745 its establishment consisted of one grenadier and ten fusilier companies, totalling about 1,500 men.

At the beginning of the period there were only three Hungarian regiments: Leopold Pálffy (no. 19), Kökenyesdy de Vettes (no. 34) and Gyulay (no. 51). In 1741 the Hungarian government proposed the formation of 13 more, but difficulties with recruiting reduced the number to six. Latin being the official language of the Hungarian government, these units were styled by the name of 'Legion', with Roman titles for the officers: *Colonellus* for *Obrist*, *Vice-Colonellus* for *Obristlieutenant*, and *Supremus Vigiliarum Praefectus* for *Obristwachtmeister*. Even the names and titles of officers were recorded officially in Latin: thus the *Colonellus* of the 6th Legion, Count Wolfgang Bethlén, was recorded as 'Comes Wolf-gangus Bethlén'. Each 'Legion' comprised one garrison and three field battalions, each of five fusilier companies. Each company consisted of one *Hauptmann*, one *Lieutenant*, one *Fähnrich*, one *Feldwäbel*,

Above: 'German' grenadiers, including an oπ cer (right: note his decorated waist pouch worn beneath the Feldbinde). The undulating lace on the cap bags is more elaborate than shown in some contemporary sources. From the ∫leur-de-lys turnback badges, presumably the regiment depicted is Deutschmeister (no. 4). (Print after R. von Ottenfeld)

'German' infantry: a fusilier company, with the oπ cer at its head bearing a partizan. (Print after R. von Ottenfeld)

one *Fourier*, one *Führer*, six *Corporals*, three drummers, three *Fourierschützen*, 12 *Gefreiters*, and 121 privates. In 1744 both old and new Hungarian regiments were put onto the standard footing of four battalions of five companies each, with about 3,000 men per regiment; the 1st–6th Legions became the regiments which bore the 1769 numbers 32, 33, 2, 31, 37 and 52 respectively.

An Invalid Regiment of four battalions was raised during the Seven Years' War, and seven Invalid companies in the Netherlands. A Garrison Regiment existed 1760–63, and three more were created subsequently, the 1st in 1766 and 2nd in 1767; these ranked as nos. 5 and 6 in the 1769 list. A 3rd Garrison Regiment was formed as a battalion in the Netherlands in 1772, and expanded to regimental strength in 1776. Light infantry duties were performed by the *Grenz* (border) regiments which, although quite distinctive, occupied the numbers 60 to 76 inclusive in the 1769 list. (They, and the various *Freicorps*, will be covered in Part 3 of this study.)

Tactics

The Austrian infantry operated according to the usual conventions of 18th century warfare, but a number of factors were peculiar to this army.

Although instructions and tactical manuals had existed before, not until 1749 was a universal manual issued to replace the various systems adopted by individual generals or regimental commanders. Only marginally revised in 1769, the 1749 regulations provided drills and routines for almost all occasions; but while including much that was unnecessary, they ignored light infantry drill for the regular regiments; and by ordering everything so exactly they perhaps tended to impair the flexibility often required on the battlefield. For example, they included a lengthy drill for the use of the half-pike or 'swine-feather' which had been used at the turn of the century but which by the 1740s was totally redundant; and many varieties of musketry drill for every conceivable circumstance, despite the fact that in action firing almost always deteriorated into a much less ordered fusillade.

Writing of the abilities of the Austrian army in the later period, a British commentator stated that

their system 'rests wholly upon discipline, science, and order', presenting 'a magnificent spectacle to military eyes'. Although the infantry was able 'to sustain a regular and open fire from the line', with 'that moral and physical immobility which, without being affected, can see whole ranks swept off by the cannon', it was suggested that this precision was achieved only at the expense of flexibility. Thus if 'dismay and confusion' took hold the troops would be 'thrown into disorder', and once scattered would be impossible to reform quickly. Furthermore, 'they carry their fear of being out-flanked to a degree which is ridiculous and extravagant; it might indeed be called a national disorder or weakness'.

For manoeuvre, a battalion was divided into 16 platoons, the strength of which varied according to circumstance, which could operate individually, in half-divisions or divisions (two and four platoons respectively). These were tactical rather than organizational units, and the term 'division' could be applied not only to a company as above, but to a two-

Obristwachtmeister *of 'German' infantry. (Print after R. von Ottenfeld)*

company unit; for example, the two regimental grenadier companies might together be styled a 'grenadier division'. Movement was normally performed in a variety of columnar formations, and combat in line. Until 1757 lines were normally composed of four ranks (grenadiers in three), and from that date in three ranks.

When firing, the front rank dropped onto the right knee, allowing the second rank to fire over their heads; the third rank could fire between the heads of the second rank by taking half a pace to one side. Where it existed, a fourth rank remained in reserve; and a tactic employed by grenadiers and Hungarians was to withdraw their rear rank and use it to assail the enemy from the flanks. Although maintenance of fire discipline in action was difficult for any troops, Austrian infantry were trained to fire either by sub-

units, from platoon upwards, or by ranks, so that either a continuous fusillade or a 'rolling volley' along the frontage of a unit was possible.

Despite the fact that grenadiers, when serving with their parent regiment, might precede the regiment from their normal position on the flanks, little training was given in anything which resembled skirmishing; although there was a tactic styled 'hedgerow-fire' employed against enemy troops sheltering behind trees or hedges (as skirmishers did), which involved a rolling volley by one platoon after another. Considerable importance was placed upon the advance with the bayonet; but only on rare occasions did hand-to-hand fighting result, as one side or the other was likely to give way before contact, to which end the front rank of an advancing unit was expected to deliver a volley before reaching the enemy.

UNIFORM AND EQUIPMENT

Initially, much of the minutiae of uniform and equipment was governed by the preferences of the regimental *Inhaber* or commanding officer; but their influence declined, especially after 1766 when Lacy became president of the *Hofkriegsrath* and ordered that supplies be drawn from central magazines. Regimental distinctions did not necessarily remain constant throughout the period and are often evident only from contemporary pictures, the minor changes of style and distinction resulting in conflicting information being shown by different sources. A further complication is the fact that many of the contemporary coloured uniform-charts showed figures in so small a scale that the minor uniform distinctions are not evident.

At the beginning of the period the items issued to every man included: every 12 years, a musket and bayonet; every eight years, a cartridge box; every five years, a knapsack; every four years, a coat; every two

Pioneer (Zimmermann) of 'German' infantry; these men wore grenadier uniform, with the addition of a leather apron and waist pouch, and carried an axe. Note the crossed axes device borne upon the cap plate. (Print after R. von Ottenfeld)

years, a waistcoat and hat; and every year, a pair of cloth breeches, two shirts and a pair of shoes.

For regular regiments the coat was white, a colour originating with the pearl-grey shade of undyed wool as worn at the beginning of the 18th century; indeed, coats were still delivered in this colour and then pipeclayed by the soldier. Although not the most practical colour for active service, blemishes could be concealed by more pipeclay, and white remained the distinctive national colour throughout the 19th century. The cut of the coat varied (some regiments, for example, favoured the tighter Prussian style), but was generally similar for all. Facing colours were displayed upon the cuffs and lapels, and for a few units on narrow folding collars; most infantry coats had no collar. The cuffs were generally quite deep, with three buttons near the upper edge. The lapels, folded back to reveal the waistcoat, bore buttons in varied arrangements, latterly mostly having seven buttons, one over two groups of three. The coat skirts were turned back, originally displaying facing-coloured lining, but as the period progressed most regiments adopted white turnbacks, sometimes fastened with buttons, tabs or distinctive regimental devices. A strap at the rear of the left shoulder was sometimes in the facing colour.

A white, long-skirted waistcoat was worn under the coat, either single- or double-breasted; latterly the double-breasted version seems to have predominated. Breeches were usually white (some coloured examples are recorded early in the period), and worn with long gaiters. These were originally white, commonly with black buttons, with black gaiters worn on active service; and from May 1754 the white gaiters were reserved officially for parade, with black (usually with brass buttons) being specified for use in wet weather and on the march. References occur to gaiters having leather tops, but these are rarely depicted clearly in contemporary pictures, though they appear in at least one of David Morier's paintings. White stockings were worn underneath the gaiters, appearing most clearly in contemporary pictures which show the use of coloured breeches, so that the tops of the stockings are clearly visible above the upper edge of the gaiters. 'German' regiments wore low shoes, commonly fastened by a buckled strap over the top of the foot.

The headdress for fusiliers was a black felt tri-

'German' infantry equipment, including 1754 musket, cartridge box and belt with brass double-eagle plate, canteen, waist belt and bayonet scabbard; with an NCO's sabre, cane and Kurzgewehr. (Print after R. von Ottenfeld)

corn hat, usually worn with the front corner inclined over the left eye, with a white lace edging (scalloped for some regiments), with a black cockade at the left secured by a lace loop and button. At the side corners were bosses or tassels in regimental colouring, and a regimentally-coloured pompon was worn by some units. On service it was usual for Austrian troops to wear a sprig of green foliage in the headdress, the *Feldzeichen* or 'field-sign', used to distinguish friend from foe in the days before the development of national uniforms. In the mid-18th century its use was not restricted to the Austrian army, but they retained it longer than any other – well into the 20th century, even though its functional use had long been redundant.

For special occasions, parades or combat, grenadiers wore bearskin caps. Of conical shape, with a low rear lined with cloth, grenadier caps had a hanging cloth 'bag', commonly of the facing colour, ornamented with lace, usually of the button-colour; many later reconstructions show this applied in undulating lines, but many contemporary pictures show instead a simple lace edging to the bag, the end of which was ornamented with a heavy tassel. Some regiments had

Above: Hungarian fusiliers. (Print after R. von Ottenfeld)

Hungarian infantry; note the Kurzgewehr 'piled' with the muskets in the background. (Print after R von Ottenfeld)

16

plain caps, others with grenade badges on the front, or metal plates with coloured cloth or enamel backing.

The hair was worn in a long, unpowdered 'queue' at the rear, and usually in rolls at the temples, although these were not commonly worn by grenadiers, to enable the fur cap to sit squarely on the head, just over the eyes; instead their side-hair was either cut short or, according to some contemporary pictures, braided into Hungarian-style locks falling from the temples. Moustaches were worn by the rank and file (not usually by officers of 'German' regiments), some of which may have been styled according to regimental practice: contemporary illustrations show waxed and upswept moustaches, more drooping styles, or even what appear to be moustaches running into sideburns. Those unable to grow adequate moustaches had to provide false ones, and it is conceivable that some regiments endeavoured to produce uniformity by making false moustaches the norm.

A fabric stock was worn around the neck; it has been stated that red stocks were worn by 'German' regiments and black by Hungarians, but contemporary illustrations show some 'Germans' with black, even though red became the regulation colour from 1754; conceivably some regiments retained black stocks for certain orders of dress. When off duty or performing manual work a forage cap could be worn, a simple cloth headdress made from old coats; in cold weather it could be worn under the ordinary hat or cap.

Equipment was of whitened leather, including a wide belt over the left shoulder supporting a black leather cartridge box at the right hip. A second belt was worn around the waist beneath the coat, from which was suspended the bayonet in a frog. Grenadiers commonly wore a smaller black cartridge box at the front of the waist, often on a narrower, separate waist belt; most grenadiers also carried a brass match case on the front of the shoulder belt, a relic of the time when they were armed with hand grenades. Metal fittings carried on the equipment were not of a universal pattern; some shoulder belts are depicted with brass buckles and sliders on the front, and

cartridge box badges, generally of grenade shape for grenadiers, were not universal. A narrower belt over the right shoulder supported the knapsack at the left rear; originally these were of fabric, but from a period before the Seven Years' War knapsacks were usually made of calfskin. A drum or ovoid-shaped canteen was carried on service.

Fusiliers carried only bayonets from the waist belt frog, but grenadiers had curved sabres in addition; *Prima Plana* NCOs (who were not armed with muskets) generally carried a sword (*Degen*) until 1748, and a version of the grenadier sabre thereafter. The design of grenadier sabre was unregulated, but generally it had a blade of about 75cm in length, brass stirrup hilt with single knuckle-bow, and a leather scabbard. The sword knot was leather or leather and

Hungarian fusilier; an early print which shows how the hat might be worn with the front 'corner' angled markedly to one side.

17

fabric, of black, brown or white, but is not shown in all contemporary pictures; a coloured fabric pad, to keep moisture out of the scabbard, is sometimes depicted around the base of the blade.

To improve comfort on the march, in 1769 it was permitted officially for the waist belt and sword to be worn over the shoulder, a practice not unique to the Austrian army and probably permitted before that date. Similarly, the waistcoat was allowed to be unfastened partially, and the stock tied around the arm; and on service in cold weather the coat-lapels could be fastened across the body and the cuffs lowered to cover the hand. Although some regiments favoured tighter coats, some were almost as voluminous as greatcoats, and on occasion were removed in action to free movement of the limbs.

Initially, the infantry's musket was the 1722-pattern *ordinäre Flinte* copied from the French 1717 pattern: 157cm overall (excluding the triangular-sectioned bayonet), with a calibre of 18.3mm. From late 1744 iron ramrods began to replace the more fragile wooden type, and the 1744 *ordinäre Fusilier-flinte* had a reduced length of 150cm. A lighter weapon of the same dimensions was tried in 1748 but was too fragile, so its best features were incorporated into the 1754 *ordinäre Commissflinte*, which unlike the 1722 pattern had the barrel secured by bands instead of pins through the stock. Fittings were iron (iron or brass before), and the sling and waterproof lock cover of white leather (white or brown earlier); the stock was stained black or dark brown for fusiliers, and of polished walnut for grenadiers. Almost the same dimensions (length 151cm) were retained for the 1767 *ordinäre Commissflinte* and 1774 *Infanterie-Gewehr*. Of the 40 rounds (or less) usually carried by the soldier, six were of buckshot for use at close range.

NCOs wore a similar uniform to that of the rank and file, generally with gold or silver hat lace for senior NCOs and corporals respectively. An early practice had been for NCOs to wear coats in 're-versed colours', but this had been replaced by the use of red or blue waistcoats according to the regimental facing-colour, a practice which appears to have de-clined during the 1740s. NCOs carried a cane, nor-mally suspended from a coat button; but as no firearm was carried by the ranks of *Feldwäbel*, *Führer*, *Fourier*, *Corporal* or *Feldscher*, they had no cartridge box or belt. Swords were carried by NCOs, with silk or wool knots (sometimes recorded as red and yel-low), but for fusiliers their principal weapon was a half-pike or *Kurzgewehr*. This is shown either as a halberd with ornately shaped axe blade and plain or wavy-edged spearhead, on a two-metre shaft; or with a plain spearhead with curved or wavy-edged blade, the latter sometimes depicted as used by corporals. Use of the *Kurzgewehr* was suspended in March 1759.

Drummers and fifers originally wore coloured coats, generally of the facing colour, but by the later 1750s it appears that regulations of 1755 had been implemented; these decreed that they should wear

Hungarian officer, wearing low shoes instead of the hussar boots which are often depicted. (Print after R. von Ottenfeld)

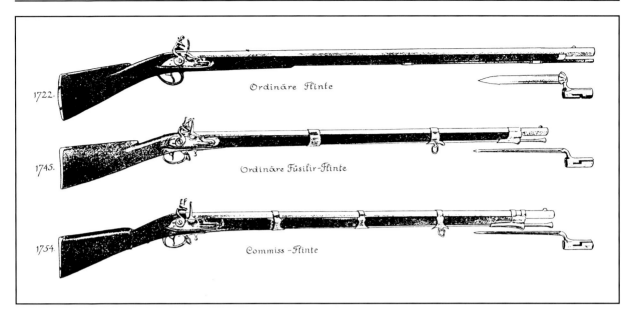

Austrian muskets: the patterns of 1722 top, 1745 centre, and 1754 bottom. (Print after R. von Ottenfeld)

ordinary uniform with the addition of laced 'swallows'-nest' style wings – supposedly these were facing-coloured with button-coloured lace, but white wings are indicated by some sources. As they carried no muskets, musicians wore neither cartridge box nor belt.

Officers' uniforms were similar to those of the other ranks but in finer material, with the coat skirts not turned back. White neck-cloths seem to have been universal; and rank distinctions were restricted to metallic hat lace and the waist sash (*Feldbinde*) of gold with interwoven black lines, the colours of the imperial arms. During the brief reign of Charles VII as emperor (1743–45) the sash was changed to grass green with gold and silver interweaving (according to regimental button-colour), and upon the reintroduction of the imperial pattern, gold lace was restricted to general officers; field officers wore sashes of yellow and black silk, and lower ranks of camel hair. Grenadier officers wore fur caps, and were armed with curved sabres and muskets; their cartridge box, worn at the front of the waist, was frequently decorated, e.g. of red leather with metallic lace edging and bearing an imperial eagle. Fusilier officers carried straight-bladed swords with a single knuckle-bow and metallic lace knot, and partizans with blackened two-metre shafts and blades graded according to rank. For *Lieutenants* the partizan head was plain; for *Hauptmann* the blade was engraved with the imperial arms, with a fabric tassel below the head, with gold or silver interwoven; for *Obristlieutenant* the blade and ferrule were gilded, and the tassel gold and silver; for *Obrist* the head was gilded and silvered, and the tassel larger. *Obristwachtmeisters* carried no partizan; and *Fähnrichs* had a *Springstock*, a half-pike with leaf-shaped head engraved with the imperial arms. The use of partizans was suspended in March 1759.

A tradition concerning officers' gloves was said to have arisen after Haddik's raid on Berlin in 1757, when he demanded from the city two dozen pairs of gloves for Maria Theresa. It was said that Haddik was tricked, as the gloves supplied were all for the left hand; supposedly this was the origin of the practice adopted by Austrian officers of carrying the right glove, so as not to appear better than their empress by having both hands covered.

Hungarian regiments

Initially Hungarian regiments wore a distinctive national costume, the general style of which is shown as Plate D1. It was very similar to hussar uniform, including a felt or fur cap, short braided jacket, pantaloons and barrelled sash; all carried a sabre and wore their hair in hussar style, with a queue at the rear and braids hanging from the temples. For the six 'Legions' formed in 1741, basic uniform details are given here, together with the name of their *Inhaber*:

Primam' (1st Legion, Forgách)

Blue coat and breeches with red braid and yellow buttons, red stock, red sash with seven blue knots (barrels), cap (*Czako-hauben*) with red trim, black leather sabretache with red face, blue Hungarian cloak, black leather cartridge box.

'Secundam' (2nd Legion, Andrássy)

Dark blue coat and breeches, yellow braid and buttons, cap with yellow trim, yellow sash with 17 blue knots, black leather sabretache with blue face, pearl grey German-style greatcoat (*Roquelor*) with blue braid.

'Tertiam' (3rd Legion, Ujváry)

Dark blue coat and breeches, yellow braid and buttons, cap with blue trim, yellow sash with blue barrels, yellow leather sabretache with blue face, white Hungarian cloak.

'Quartam' (4th Legion, Haller)

Light blue coat and breeches, red braid and sash, white or yellow buttons, cap with red trim, yellow leather sabretache with red leather face, yellow leather cartridge box, white Hungarian cloak.

'Quintam' (5th Legion, Szirmay)

Light blue coat and breeches, red braid, white buttons, cap with white trim, red sash with white barrels, red sabretache and cartridge box, white Hungarian cloak.

'Sextam' (6th Legion, Bethlén)

Blue coat and breeches, red braid, yellow buttons, cap with blue trim, red sash with blue barrels, red sabretache with blue face, red leather cartridge box, blue Hungarian cloak with red braid.

Officers wore hussar uniform, including a peakless felt *Czako-hauben* with gold lace around the upper edge, blue dolman and breeches and white pelisse with gold braid and gilt buttons, sash with gold barrels and sabretache with gold decoration; and carried muskets. The rank and file wore laced ankle boots, but officers had hussar boots; Knötel shows e.g. an officer of Regt. Ujváry (3rd Legion, later regt. no. 2) with yellow boots.

Hungarian uniform was regulated later, and from 1748–49 the white coat became standard. It had facing-coloured turnbacks and cuffs, the latter usually pointed (but flat-topped for regts. 39 and 51), but

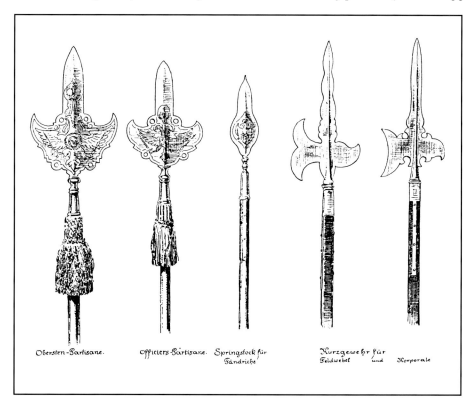

Polearms: officers' partizans (left, *the pattern for Obrist having a larger head and tassel*), NCOs' **Kurzgewehr** *in two typical styles*, right, *and* Fähnriche's Springstock, centre.

no lapels; on each side of the breast were lace troops, often with tassel ends, usually set one over two over three, but this spacing was not universal: e.g. Morier shows Regts. Haller and Bethlén (nos. 31 and 52) with six loops on each side, in pairs. The headdress was like that of 'German' regiments, but the Hungarian hair-style was retained. Beneath the coat was worn a braided, hussar-style dolman and barrelled sash, and legwear remained distinctive: tight pantaloons, generally blue, tucked into laced ankle boots. An early style was the use of coloured cloth *scharawaden* (thigh-length stockings or over-trousers) worn over buff breeches, and such was the emulation of hussar uniform that some Hungarian infantry even carried sabretaches.

Equipment was like that of 'German' regiments, but all carried sabres suspended from narrow waist belts of hussar style; Morier shows Regt. Ujváry (no. 2) with two narrow waist belts, one each for sabre and bayonet. Other varieties are also depicted, for example a narrow brown shoulder belt shown in Morier's painting of Regt. Bethlén (no. 52). The pattern of sabre was unregulated initially (Morier, for example, shows Regt. Haller (no. 31) with a mameluke-style hilt with no knuckle-bow), but from 1748 it was supposed to have a 66cm blade, brass mounts, and wood and leather scabbard; those carried by NCOs were much more decorative and cost twice as much as those of privates.

Officers of Hungarian regiments wore a similar uniform, but with metallic lace decoration and hussar boots; they carried sabres, and instead of the ordinary *Feldbinde* wore black and yellow (or gold) barrelled sashes. Among variations, Knötel shows an officer of Regt. Josef Esterházy (no. 37) in a white coat with red collar, pointed cuffs and turnbacks, blue dolman and breeches with silver braid, silver-laced hussar boots, red and silver barrelled sash, and a mirliton-style winged cap, edged with silver lace, with a white plume and silver 'raquettes' at the left.

The 1767 uniform

The sabre having been proved useful in the recent campaigns, from 1765 it was issued to all infantry. For fusiliers it had a slightly curved 53cm blade, wood and leather scabbard, and brass mounts, including a pommel, backstrap and short quillons, but no knuckle-bow. For grenadiers and lower NCOs it

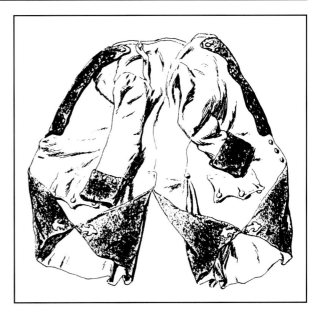

'German' infantry coat, pre-1767; the arrangement of buttons in three groups of three on each lapel is unusual. (Print after R. von Ottenfeld)

had a 58cm blade and a brass hilt with a knuckle-bow, *Prima Plana* ranks carrying a similar weapon with gilded fittings and lionhead pommel. The blade length was increased to 67cm from 1777. Sword knots were gold or silver for officers, with spangles for field ranks, white or yellow wool for NCOs, and silk for cadets and *Prima Plana* ranks, according to the button colour.

A major change in uniform style occurred in 1767, perhaps at the personal instigation of Maria Theresa, who was always greatly concerned for the welfare of her troops. The new single-breasted coat was shorter and less voluminous than that worn before, and was worn fastened across the breast (although occasionally shown open in contemporary illustrations, exposing the waistcoat). It was white, with a small folding collar, turnbacks and round cuffs in the facing colour, with horizontal pockets and a strap at the rear of the left shoulder. New facing colours were authorized, involving a much wider range of shades than before, as follows:

Pompadour (dark red) for regts. nos. 1, 18; Imperial yellow (*kaisergelb*: dark yellow) 2, 22, 27, 31; sapphire blue 3, 4, 19; dark blue 7, 24, 33, 46, 51; poppy red 8, 23; apple green 9, 54; parrot green 10, 26; rose red 11, 38; dark brown 12; grass green 13, 28; black 14, 58; red 15 (madder 1778), 37, 39, 52; violet

16, 50; sulphur yellow 17, 43; crab red 20, 35; sea green 21, 25; light blue 29, 55; pike grey 30, 49; sky blue 32, 41; *grisdelin* (lilac grey) 36; madder red 34, 44; carmine 40, 45, 57; orange-yellow 42, 59; steel green 47, 56; light brown 48; dark red 53. Buttons were white for nos. 3, 7, 10, 11, 17–20, 21 (1778 yellow), 22–25, 28, 29, 31, 33, 34, 36, 39–42, 47, 49, 50, 53, 54 and 58; and yellow for the remainder. Some published material suggests variations in the above; and in 1770 Regt. no. 17 changed facings from sulphur yellow to light brown, and no. 41 from sky blue to sulphur yellow, the latter at the instigation of the *Inhaber*, Prince Furstenberg.

For the rank and file the tricorn was replaced by the *Casquet*, a squat, flat-topped cap with rounded leather false front bound with scalloped white lace (silver for NCOs), bearing a brass plate embossed with the imperial cypher, and a yellow pompon with black centre at the left side. The lace was removed in 1780, and the plate's cypher changed to 'J II'. Officers continued to wear the tricorn; their single-breasted coat was worn with a facing-coloured waist-coat. 'German' regiments continued to wear white breeches and black gaiters; Hungarian regiments wore blue pantaloons and laced ankle boots, and a further distinction was the use of pointed coat cuffs

bearing a fringed loop of button-coloured lace. The grenadier cap was restyled so that the bag no longer hung down at the side or rear, and had a brass plate. A grey greatcoat was issued from this date, single-breasted with six buttons set one over two over three; deep cuffs; a low collar, and a shoulder strap at the left, both piped in the facing colour. Musicians were distinguished by facing-coloured 'swallow's-nest' wings, edged with undulating white lace and bearing a rosette of the same lace in the centre, with similar lace edging the collar and cuffs.

Foreign regiments

Austria maintained a number of foreign regiments, some of which were hired from obliging states. These included the two regiments taken from the service of the Bishop of Würzburg in September 1757, known from the colour of their facings as Blau-Würzburg and Roth-Würzburg; their uniform and organization were basically of Austrian style. Italian units included the Tuscan Regiment, taken over in 1757 (Maria Theresa's husband being the Grand Duke of Tuscany), one cavalry and three infantry regiments hired in the same year from Modena.

A different type of foreign corps was the *Reichsarmee*, which although not strictly Austrian

Infantry equipment
c. 1770, including knapsack
with rolled greatcoat on
top, the changing patterns
of Casquet, the 1765
fusilier sabre and bayonet
in a combined frog, and
NCO sabre. (Print after R.
von Ottenfeld)

was part of the Imperial military force. The Holy Roman Empire was divided into ten regions or *Kreis* (lit. 'circle'), the states of which were obliged to provide troops for the defence of the empire. The resulting regiments were generally of poor quality, badly equipped and sometimes virtually untrained. A few regiments supplied by a single state were generally good troops – the Hessen-Darmstadt Regiment of the Upper Rhine *Kreis* was an excellent corps; but the majority of regiments were composed of small contingents from a number of states, even as many as 40 contingents within one regiment. This hardly made for a cohesive body, and even resulted in different uniforms being worn within the same corps. Many *Reichsarmee* regiments were organized and equipped in Austrian style, but others followed Prussian fashions; indeed, in 1757 blue coats predominated among the imperial infantry, only nine out of 45 battalions wearing the Austrian white. These troops would probably have been adequate for garrison or internal security duties, but in the field the *Reichsarmee* was of little use (with a few honourable exceptions), as demonstrated by their conduct at Rossbach.

INFANTRY REGIMENTS

Regiments are listed below according to the numbers allocated in 1769; those disbanded before that date are listed in the alphabetical order of the names of their *Inhaber* in 1740, or their first *Inhaber* if raised after that date. Regiments numbered 60 onwards were *Grenz* corps, to be covered in Part 3 of this study. Regiments were recruited within the empire unless a more precise area is given in parentheses after the number. Unless stated otherwise, the brief uniform details are those applicable to the period of the Seven Years' War, c. 1762, though some earlier descriptions are included by way of comparison. Conflicting information exists concerning some of the minor regimental distinctions, which might not have been constant throughout the period.

Fusilier in greatcoat; the Casquet *is the 1780 style, without the original lace decoration. (Print after R. von Ottenfeld)*

The term 'rosette' used below describes the decoration at the corners of the hat; the pompon is also that worn on the hat.

No. 1 (Empire and Moravia)

Titles: 1740 Lothringen (i.e. Lorraine); *Inhaber* was Francis Stephen, Maria Theresa's husband. Title was originally 'Erbprinz von Lothringen' (1726),

then 'Herzog zu Lothringen' (1729); titled 'Kaiser' from 1745 when Francis Stephen became emperor, which title was retained in 1765 when Joseph II succeeded his father as emperor and *Inhaber*.
Uniform: Red facings (including waistcoat, turn-backs, collar 1757), yellow buttons, shoulder strap white or white piped red; pompon black and yellow, or black/yellow/red, rosettes same, or yellow.

No. 2 (Hungarian)
Titles: Raised in western Hungary 1741; 1741 Ujváryi (or Ujvary), 1749 Erzherzog Carl, 1761 Erzherzog Ferdinand.
Uniform: See Plates D2 and E3.

No. 3
Titles: Carl von Lothringen (i.e. Prince Charles of Lorraine); titled thus from 1736, Erzherzog Carl from 1780.
Uniform: Red facings (including waistcoat and turnbacks 1757), yellow buttons, shoulder strap and turnback tabs yellow with red piping (Ottenfeld indicates white, piped red); scalloped hat-lace, pompon red/yellow/blue from outside, red rosettes; or red and green with light blue rosettes.

No. 4
Title: Deutschmeister (or 'Hoch- und Deutsch-meister'), from the Grand Master and master of the German chapter of the Teutonic Order, who was *Inhaber*. Regiment formed 1696 from the household troops of the then Grand Master, Franz Ludwig of Pfalz–Neuberg. This crusading order of chivalry was formed in the 12th century, and from the 16th century had its headquarters at Mergentheim in Swabia, a holding of about 15,000 German square

Above: 'German' grenadiers, c. 1778. (Print after Adolph Menzel)

'German' grenadiers on the march, with waterproof-covered caps, c. 1770. (Print after R. von Ottenfeld)

1: Grenadier, Regt. Los Rios, c. 1748
2: Grenadier, Regt. Waldeck, c. 1748
3: Officer, Regt. Moltke, c. 1750

WRV. 94

A

1: Feldwäbel, Regt. Thürheim, c. 1757
2: Field officer, Regt. Salm-Salm, c. 1760
3: Fusilier, Regt. Ligne, c. 1759

B

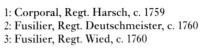

1: Corporal, Regt. Harsch, c. 1759
2: Fusilier, Regt. Deutschmeister, c. 1760
3: Fusilier, Regt. Wied, c. 1760

C

1: Private, Regt. Kökenyésdy de Vettes, 1742
2: Grenadier, Regt. Ujváryi, c. 1748
3: Grenadier, Regt. Haller, c. 1748

WRY. 94

D

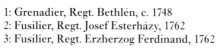
1: Grenadier, Regt. Bethlén, c. 1748
2: Fusilier, Regt. Josef Esterházy, 1762
3: Fusilier, Regt. Erzherzog Ferdinand, 1762

WRy. 94

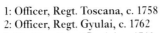

1: Officer, Regt. Toscana, c. 1758
2: Officer, Regt. Gyulai, c. 1762
3: Fusilier, Regt. Gyulai, c. 1762
4: Fusilier, Regt. Hall~ , c. 1762

WRJ. 94

F

1: Hungarian grenadier, 1767 uniform
2: 'German' fusilier, 1767 uniform
3: 'German' fusilier drummer, 1767 uniform

WRY. 94

G

1: Fusilier, Anhalt-Zerbst Bn., 1761
2: Grenadier, Mainz Kreis-contingent, 1757
3: Grenadier, Hessen-Darmstadt Kreis-contingent, 1757

H

miles. Although the Grand Master was a prince of the empire, there was no firmer association with Austria until the emperor of Austria was invested as Grand Master by the Treaty of Pressburg (1805). Recruiting for this regiment was centred in the lands of the Order.
Uniform: See Plate C2.

No. 5
Title: 1st Garrison Regt., formed from invalids 1766.
Uniform: Dark blue facings, white buttons.

No. 6
Title: 2nd Garrison Regt., formed 1767.
Uniform: Black facings, yellow buttons.
(A 3rd Garrison Regt. was formed as a battalion in 1772, expanded to a regiment in 1776; it served in the Netherlands and wore black facings and white buttons).

No. 7
Titles: 1740 Neipperg, 1774 Harrach.
Uniform: Blue facings 1740, red 1743, blue 1748, yellow buttons (Knötel indicates white), facing-coloured or white shoulder strap; red pompon with yellow centre (Ottenfeld indicates vice-versa), yellow and black rosettes; other sources indicate neither pompon nor rosettes.

No. 8
Title: Sachsen-Hildburghausen (the prince of Saxe-Hildburghausen was *Inhaber*).
Uniform: Red facings (including waistcoat and turnbacks 1757), yellow buttons, white shoulder

The officers' version of the 1767 uniform, centre, is illustrated in this print after R. von Ottenfeld, including a single-breasted white coat and facing-coloured waistcoat. The private, left, wears the uniform reserved for work or undress, waistcoat, shirt, breeches and stockings, and a simple cloth forage cap.

strap; some sources indicate a black stock; red rosettes (Albertina MS indicates rosette on right side only).

No. 9 (Netherlands)
Titles: 1740 Los Rios (or 'Los Rios de Gutierez'), 1775 Clerfayt.
Uniform: Apple green facings, white or facing-coloured shoulder strap, yellow buttons; red and yellow rosettes. See also Plate A1.

No. 10 (South-western Germany)
Title: Braunschweig-Wolfenbüttel (the prince of that state was *Inhaber;* known as 'Jung-Wolfenbüttel' to distinguish it from no. 29).
Uniform: Red facings, yellow buttons; shoulder straps recorded as white with red piping, red, or white; pompon light blue with yellow ring, or light blue; rosettes blue and red or light blue and white.

No. 11
Title: Wallis (Franz Wenzel, Graf von Wallis was *Inhaber* from 1739; M.J. von Wallis 1774).
Uniform: Red facings 1740, blue 1743, red 1748, white buttons and shoulder strap; red and yellow rosettes.

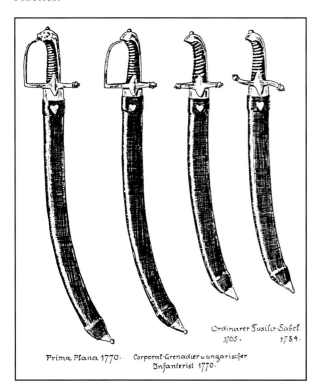

Prima Plana 1770.   Corporal-Grenadier u ungarischer
Infanterist 1770.

Ordinarer Fusilir-Sabel
1765.   1784.

No. 12
Titles: 1740 Botta d'Adorno, 1775 Khevenhüller-Metsch.
Uniform: Blue facings (including waistcoat and turnbacks 1757), shoulder straps; yellow buttons; blue pompon with white centre, or blue with white ring; rosettes yellow and red, or blue and white.

No. 13 (Austrian Alps)
Titles: 1740 Moltke, 1780 Zettwitz; the oldest of the infantry regiments, raised 1630.
Uniform: See Plate A3.

No. 14
Titles: 1740 Salm-Salm, 1770 Ferraris, 1775 Tillier.
Uniform: See Plate B2.

No. 15
Titles: 1740 Pallavicini, 1773 Fabris.
Uniform: Facings blue 1740, red 1757, yellow buttons, red shoulder strap piped mixed red and white (Ottenfeld indicates white strap with this edging), red turnback patch edged white (not indicated by Ottenfeld); red pompon with white centre and ring: rosettes yellow, or red and white.

No. 16
Titles: 1740 Livingstein, 1741 Königsegg-Rothenfels, 1778 Terzy.
Uniform: Dark blue or violet-blue facings and shoulder strap (Ottenfeld indicates blue collar and white cuffs), yellow buttons, blue dart-shaped turnback badge (not indicated by Ottenfeld); rosettes red and yellow, or red and blue.

No. 17
Titles: 1740 Kollowrat-Krakowsky, 1773 Koch.
Uniform: Red facings (including waistcoat and turnbacks 1757), red shoulder strap piped white, red dart-shaped turnback badge piped yellow, yellow buttons; yellow pompon with red ring, red and yellow rosettes.

Infantry sabres: the grenadier and Hungarian version with a plain knuckle-bow, the Prima Plana *version with lion-head pommel, and the 1765 fusilier sabre with the original straight quillon, and the curving quillon of 1784. (Print after R. von Ottenfeld)*

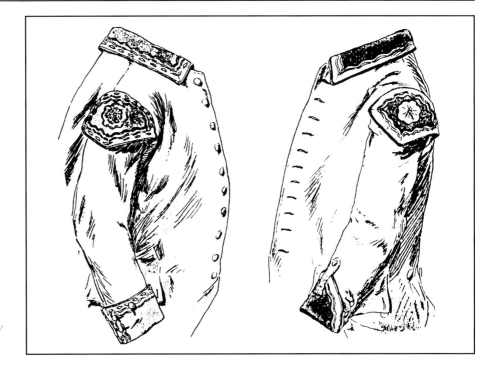

Right: 'German' drummer's coat, 1767 pattern, showing the undulating lace on collar, cuffs and wings. (Print after R. von Ottenfeld)

Far right: Hungarian drummer's coat, 1767 pattern, showing the pointed Hungarian cuff with fringed lace loop. (Print after R. von Ottenfeld)

Below: 'German' infantry coat, 1767 pattern. (Print after R. von Ottenfeld)

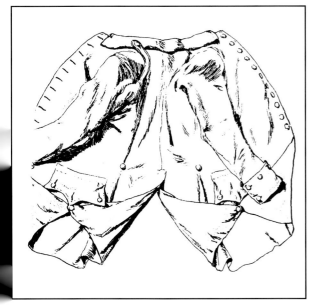

No. 18

Titles: 1740 Seckendorff, 1742 Marshal von Biberstein (or 'Marchal'), 1773 Brinken (or 'Brincken').

Uniform: Red facings (including turnbacks 1757), shoulder strap and turnback patch, yellow buttons, red and yellow rosettes.

No. 19 (Hungarian)

Titles: 1740 Leopold Pálffy, 1773 d'Alton.

Uniform: Blue facings (including waistcoat and turnbacks 1757), later indicated as light blue; yellow buttons, white turnbacks, light blue breeches; light blue braid on coat, red on waistcoat; dark red sash.

No. 20

Titles: 1740 Diesbach, 1744 Colloredo-Waldsee (or 'Kolloredo'; known as 'Alt-Colloredo' after 1754 to distinguish it from Regt. no. 40).

Uniform: Facings blue 1740, red 1743, blue 1757, yellow buttons, blue shoulder strap (or yellow; Ottenfeld indicates a very narrow blue strap), blue oblong turnback patch; blue pompon (Ottenfeld indicates white with blue centre), rosettes red and blue, or blue; yellow cypher of conjoined 'AC' carried below pompon instead of button and loop. Knötel states yellow facings from 1760, but blue recorded still in use in 1762.

No. 21

Titles: 1740 Schulenberg, 1754 Arenberg (or 'Aremberg'), 1778 Gemmingen.

Uniform: Blue facings (usually indicated as light blue), yellow buttons, white shoulder strap and turnback patch with blue border and central undulating line; scalloped hat-lace, light green pompon with white centre, green and white rosettes.

The joint cypher of Maria Theresa and her son Joseph appear on this Casquet-plate of 1767. This illustrates the often considerable delay between the issue of a regulation and its implementation: despite the introduction of two successive patterns in the intervening years, this plate was excavated from the site of the Battle of Montenotte (12 April 1796), evidence of the use of the plate some 16 years after it was superseded in 1780. (Photograph courtesy Bruno Chionetti)

No. 22

Titles: 1740 Suckow, 1741 Roth, 1748 Hagenbach, 1757 Sprecher von Bernegg, 1756 Lacy (or 'Lascy').
Uniform: Red facings (red turnbacks, blue waistcoat 1757), red or white shoulder strap, red rectangular turnback patch, yellow buttons; red pompon with yellow edge, white inner; rosettes red and yellow or red/yellow/white.

No. 23 (Baden)

Titles: 1740 Baden-Baden (Graf Ludwig of Baden-Baden was *Inhaber* from 1707, succeeded by Graf August 1761), 1771 Ried, 1779 Erzherzog Ferdinand.
Uniform: Blue facings (including turnbacks and waistcoat 1757), shoulder strap white or blue piped white, yellow buttons, blue trefoil turnback badges. The Gudenus MS shows a grenadier of 1734 with blue turnbacks, breeches, waistcoat and deep cuffs (almost concealing a vertical white flap), no badges on cap or pouches.

No. 24 (Inner Austria)

Titles: 1740 Stahremberg (Graf Max Adam was *Inhaber* 1703-41, Graf E.M. thereafter), 1771 Preiss. Second oldest of the infantry regiments, raised 1632.
Uniform: Dark blue facings (including waistcoat and turnbacks 1757), blue or white shoulder strap, blue oblong turnback patch, yellow buttons; blue or blue and white rosettes.

No. 25

Titles: 1740 Wachtendonk (or 'Wachtendonck'), 1741 Piccolomini, 1757 Thürheim (or 'Thierheim').
Uniform: See Plate B1.

No. 26 (Rhine district)

Titles: 1740 Grünne, 1751 Puebla, 1776 Riese.
Uniform: Blue facings 1740, red 1743 (including turnbacks at least until 1762), yellow buttons, shoulder strap white piped red, or red; red oblong turnback patch sometimes indicated; scalloped hat-lace, red and yellow rosette (or white pompon, black rosettes).

No. 27

Titles: 1740 Hessen-Cassel, 1753 Baden-Durlach (the princes of both these states being *Inhaber*).
Uniform: Light blue facings (including turnbacks shown at least until 1762), shoulder strap, and oblong turnback patch (indicated by Ottenfeld on white turnbacks); red rosettes; no hat-lace indicated by Ottenfeld. The Gudenus MS shows a grenadier of 1734 (two years after Prince Max of Hessen-Cassel became *Inhaber*) with dark blue facings, turnbacks, waistcoat and breeches, blue cap-plate with rounded white upper edge and brass coat of arms, and plain pouches.

No. 28

Titles: 1740 Arenberg, 1754 Scherzen (or 'Scherzer'), 1754 Weid-Runkel, 1779 Wartensleben.
Uniform: See Plate C3.

No. 29

Titles: 1740 Braunscheig-Wolfenbüttel (or 'Alt-Wolfenbüttel'), 1760 Loudon.
Uniform: Facings red 1740, blue 1748, white shoulder strap and pointed-ended turnback patch edged blue, yellow buttons; scalloped hat-lace; some

sources indicate no pompon or rosettes, or alternatively both red and dark blue.

No. 30 (Netherlands)
Titles: 1740 Prié-Turinetti, 1753 Sachsen-Gotha (the prince of that state was *Inhaber*), 1771 Ligne (Charles Joseph, prince de Ligne).
Uniform: Blue facings 1740, red indicated 1757 (including waistcoat and turnbacks) but blue by 1762, yellow buttons, white shoulder strap with white/red/blue border (Ottenfeld indicates mixed white/red/blue strap with short fringe); red pompon and rosettes.

No. 31 (Hungarian)
Titles: Raised 1741; 1741 Haller von Hallerstein, 1777 Esterházy, 1780 Orosz.
Uniform: See Plates D3 and F4.

No. 32 (Hungarian)
Titles: Raised 1741; 1741 Forgach (or 'Forgats'), 1773 Gyulai (or 'Gyulay').
Uniform: Light blue facings (including waistcoat, breeches and turnbacks), yellow buttons, light blue lace on coat, light blue or white shoulder strap; red lace on waistcoat (Ottenfeld indicates white), white diamond-shaped turnback badges; light blue pompon (Ottenfeld, light blue with white edge), light blue rosettes.

No. 33 (Hungarian)
Titles: Raised 1741; 1741 Andrássy, 1753 Nikolaus Esterházy.
Uniform: Yellow facings 1748, dark blue by 1757 (including turnbacks, waistcoat and breeches), blue or white shoulder strap, blue lace on coat, yellow on waistcoat, yellow buttons, blue and yellow sash; yellow pompon with blue centre, rosettes blue and yellow, or blue.

No. 34 (Hungarian)
Titles: 1740 Kökényesdy de Vettes (or 'Kökemesdy de Vetés', or 'Vettes'), 1756 Batthianyi (or 'Batthyany'), 1780 A. Esterházy.
Uniform: Yellow facings (including turnbacks), dark blue by 1762, dark blue waistcoat, breeches, shoulder strap, yellow buttons, yellow lace on coat and waistcoat, yellow or blue and yellow sash.

No. 35 (Franconia and Swabia)
Titles: 1740 Waldeck, 1763 Macquire, 1767 Hessen-Darmstadt, 1774 Wallis.
Uniform: Blue facings 1738, red 1743, yellow buttons, red or white shoulder strap; red dart-shaped turnback

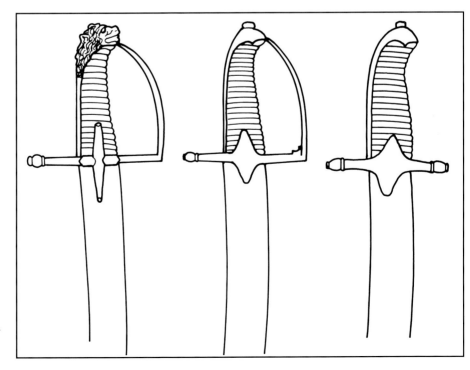

Left: Prima plana *sabre with lion-head pommel; brass hilt with black leather grip.*

Centre: Grenadier *sabre; brass hilt with black leather grip.*

Right: 1765-pattern fusilier *sabre; brass hilt with black leather grip.*

badge, or red with yellow border; red pompon and rosettes (Ottenfeld, no pompon). See Plate A2.

No. 36
Titles: 1740 Browne (Field-Marshal Maximilian Ulysses, 1737–57, mortally wounded at Prague; then Josef Browne, killed at Hochkirch), 1759 Tillier, 1761 Kinsky

Uniform: Light blue facings, white buttons; shoulder strap and rounded oblong turnback badge white with light blue edge and undulating central line; red pompon with yellow centre, rosettes red and blue or red and yellow. Morier shows a grenadier which has been identified at Regt. Browne, with green cuffs and turnbacks, no lapels, white buttons, white metal arms on waist-pouch, and a cap with pointed green plate edged white and bearing a brass grenade, and green bag with white lace and tassel.

No. 37 (Hungarian: Slovakian)
Titles: Raised 1741; 1741 Szirmay, 1744 Josef Esterházy, 1762 Siskovics.
Uniform: See Plate E2.

No. 38 (Netherlands)
Titles: 1740 Ligne (Furst Claudius), 1766 d'Aynse, 1774 Kaunitz.
Uniform: See Plate B3.

No. 39 (Hungarian)
Titles: Raised 1756; 1756 Pálffy, 1758 Preysach.
Uniform: Red facings (including breeches, waistcoat and turnbacks, though white waistcoat and breeches indicated 1757), white shoulder strap edged red, white lace on coat and waistcoat, white buttons, straight cuffs, red and white sash, white triangular turnback badge; white pompon with red centre, red rosettes (alternative indicates no pompon, yellow and black rosettes).

No. 40 (Erblanden: Habsburg 'hereditary lands')
Titles: 1740 Damnitz, 1754 Carl Colloredo (known as 'Jung-Colloredo').
Uniform: Blue facings 1740, red 1743, dark blue 1748, yellow buttons; shoulder strap white or white piped red; turnback badge dark blue interlocking

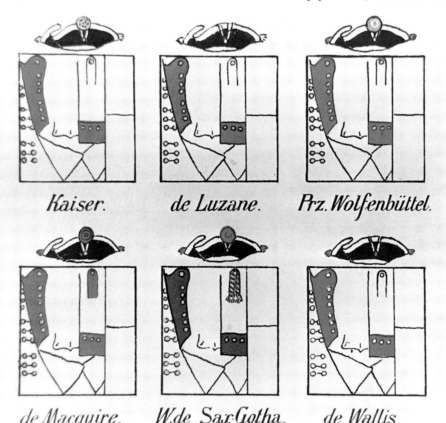

Infantry uniform, c. 1762; regiments numbered (top left to bottom right) 1, 48, 10, 46, 30 and 11; colour details in the text.

letters 'C'; white pompon with dark blue centre, rosettes blue, or blue and white.

No. 41 (Bavaria/Franconia)
Titles: 1740 Bayreuth (Friedrich, prince of), 1767 Plunquet, 1770 Carl Fürstenberg, 1777 Belgiojoso, 1778 Bender.
Uniform: Light blue facings 1740, red 1743 (including collar), yellow buttons, red shoulder strap (Ottenfeld indicates white); scalloped hat-lace; pompon green/yellow/white or green and red (Ottenfeld indicates yellow with white edge, red centre); rosettes green and red, or red and yellow.

No. 42 (Franconia)
Titles: 1740 O'Nelly, 1743 Gaisruck, 1769 Gemmingen, 1775 Mathesen.
Uniform: Facings blue 1740, red 1743, blue 1757 (including turnbacks, but white by 1762), yellow buttons; shoulder strap and rounded oblong turnback badges blue with white edge and undulating central line (white also recorded; Ottenfeld indicates white shoulder strap with blue edge and undulating

line, blue turnback badge edge white); yellow pompon with blue centre, rosettes red and blue (yellow/white, and red respectively, also recorded).

No. 43
Titles: 1740 Platz, 1768 Buttler, 1775 Thurn.
Uniform: Facings blue 1740, red 1743, red shoulder strap and turnback-oblong, yellow buttons.

No. 44 (Lombardy)
Titles: Raised 1744; 1744 Clerici, 1769 Gaisrück, 1778 Belgiojoso.
Uniform: Red facings (including shoulder strap and turnback badge, the latter recorded as heart-shaped), yellow buttons, rosettes green and yellow.

No. 45 (Moravia/Silesia)
Titles: 1740 Heinrich Daun, 1761 O'Kelly (or 'Okelli'), 1767 Bülow, 1776 Lattermann.
Uniform: Red facings, yellow buttons, red shoulder strap, red diamond-shaped turnback badge (or red with yellow edge; Ottenfeld indicates white shoulder strap and oblong turnback-tab); red pompon with yellow centre (or vice-versa), rosettes red and yellow.

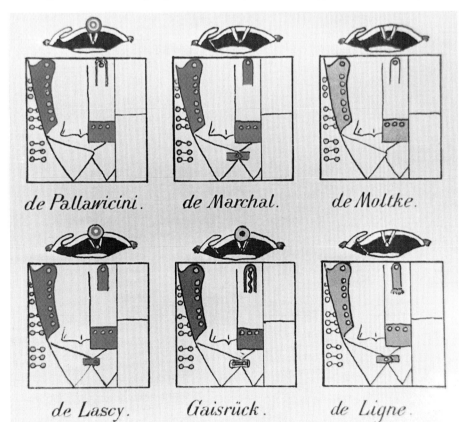

de Pallavicini.   *de Marchal.*   *de Moltke.*

de Lascy.   *Gaisrück.*   *de Ligne.*

Infantry uniform, c. 1762; regiments numbered (top left to bottom right) 15, 18, 13, 22, 42 and 38; colour details in the text.

No. 46 (Tyrol)

Titles: Tiroler Land- und Feld-Regiment, raised 1745; 1745 Spauer, 1748 Ogilvy (or 'O'Gilvy'), 1751 Sincère, 1752 Macquire, 1764 Migazzi (or 'Migazzy'). This unit was formed from the Tyrolean militia battalion (*Tiroler Land-Bataillon*) and took on the constitution of a 'German' regiment in 1748, with many recruits from outside the Tyrol, the inhabitants of which showed little enthusiasm for enlisting. In 1766 the 'native' elements were re-formed as the *Tiroler Land-Bataillon* and in 1771 the regimental establishment was increased to 6,000, of whom 2,000 were for service only in the Tyrol.

Uniform: Red facings (including turnbacks and waistcoat 1757), red shoulder strap, yellow buttons, red pennon-shaped turnback badge (not indicated by Ottenfeld); green pompon, red rosettes.

No. 47 (Silesia)

Titles: 1740 Harrach, 1764 Brandenburg-Bayreuth (or 'Bayreuth'; the Margrave of that state was *Inhaber*), 1769 Elrichshausen, 1779 Kinsky.

Uniform: 1740 blue facings, red 1743, blue 1757 (including waistcoat and turnbacks in 1757), yellow buttons, blue shoulder strap and pennon- or dart-shaped turnback badge; yellow pompon (not indicated by Ottenfeld), blue and yellow rosettes.

No. 48 (Lombardy)

Titles: 1740 Vasquez de Binas, 1755 Luzan (or 'Luzane'). 1765 Ried, 1773 Caprara.

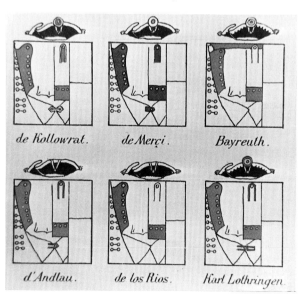

Uniform: Green facings (including waistcoat and breeches 1757), yellow buttons, white shoulder strap; Ottenfeld indicates white rosettes, not noted by other sources.

No. 49 (Baden-Durlach)

Titles: 1740 Walsegg, 1743 Bäarnklau, 1747 Kheul, 1758 Angern, 1767 Pellegrini.

Uniform: Red facings, white buttons and shoulder strap; rosettes yellow and blue, or yellow and green.

No. 50 (Bohemia)

Titles: 1740 Wurmbrand, 1749 Harsch, 1766 Poniatowski (or 'Poniatowsky'), 1773 Stain. Third oldest of the infantry regiments, raised 1642.

Uniform: Red facings (including turnbacks as late as 1762), white buttons and tassel-ended loops on lapels and cuffs, red shoulder strap with tassel-ended loop on it; blue and red rosettes. The Gudenus MS shows a grenadier of 1734 (seven years into the tenure of the *Inhaber* Wurmbrand) with red cuffs and turnbacks, white waistcoat, breeches and buttons, black stock, plain grenadier cap, and brass coats of arms on the waist pouch and cartridge box, the latter with separate grenade badges in the lower corners. Morier shows a grenadier with red folding collar, lapels, cuffs and turnbacks, white buttons; waist pouch bearing a brass grenade, worn on a separate black strap, not attached to the ordinary waist belt; and a cap with no plate but with a red bag with yellow lace and tassel.

No. 51 (Hungarian)

Title: Gyulai (or 'Gyulay' or 'Gyulaj'): Graf Stephan Gyulai was *Inhaber* from 1735, succeeded by Graf Franz Gyulai 1759. Also known as the Transylvanian National Regiment (*Siebenburgisches National-Regiment*). Oldest of the Hungarian infantry regiments, raised 1702.

Uniform: See Plate F3.

No. 52 (Hungarian)

Titles: Raised 1741; 1741 Bethlén, 1763 Károlyi (or 'Karoly').

Uniform: See Plate E1.

Infantry uniform, c. 1762; regiments numbered (top left to bottom right) 17, 56, 41, 57, 9, 3; colour details in the text.

No. 53 (Hungarian)

Titles: Formed as a line regiment from Trenck's Pandours 1756; 1756 Simbschen, 1763 Beck, 1768 Pálffy.

Uniform: Red facings (including waistcoat, breeches and turnbacks), violet or dark red tasselled loops on coat, yellow lace on waistcoat, yellow or white buttons; sash black and yellow (or black with white-and-red); scalloped hat-lace.

No. 54 (Lower Austria/Moravia)

Titles: 1740 Königsegg-Rothenfels, 1751 Sincère, 1769 Callenberg.

Uniform: Red facings, yellow buttons, shoulder strap white with red edge and central zigzag line; scalloped hat-lace, yellow pompon, yellow and red rosettes.

No. 55 (Netherlands)

Titles: Raised 1742 as 1st *Niederländisches National-Regiment*; 1742 Chanclos, 1746 Arberg (or 'D'Arberg'), 1768 Murray.

Uniform: Red facings (including waistcoat and turnbacks 1757), yellow buttons, white shoulder strap edged red; black pompon, red and yellow rosettes; recorded alternatives are red and green pompon, light blue rosettes; Ottenfeld indicates light blue pompon with red edge and yellow centre, red and white rosettes. Morier shows a grenadier with red turnbacks, waistcoat and breeches, and a red cap-plate with brass edge and grenade.

No. 56 (Silesia)

Titles: 1740 P. Daun, 1741 Merci-Argenteau (or 'Mercy'), 1767 Nugent.

Uniform: Red facings 1740, blue or violet-blue 1743, yellow buttons, blue shoulder strap and dart-shaped turnback badge; white pompon with blue centre, blue and white rosettes.

No. 57 (Saxe-Coburg)

Titles: 1740 Thüngen, 1745 Andlau, 1769 Colloredo-Waldsee (or 'Colloredo').

Uniform: Red facings, yellow buttons, white shoulder strap edged red, white dart-shaped turnback badge edged red; red and yellow rosettes.

Infantry uniform, c. 1762; regiments numbered (top left to bottom right) 24, 26, 47, 36, 8 and 20; colour details in the text.

No. 58 (Netherlands)

Title: Raised by the French and taken into Austrian service 1763; 1763 Vierset.

Uniform: Blue facings, yellow buttons.

No. 59 (Upper and Lower Austria)

Titles: 1740 Daun (Leopold Daun *Inhaber* until 1766, then Franz Daun), 1771 Langlois.

Uniform: Red facings, yellow buttons, red or white shoulder strap, red diamond turnback badge; green pompon with yellow monogram 'LD' ('Leopold Daun') below, instead of the usual lace loop, red and blue rosettes (alternatively, white pompon and red rosettes).

The following regiments were disbanded before numbers were allocated in 1769; they are listed below alphabetically according to the name of the *Inhaber* in 1740, or its first *Inhaber* if formed after that date:

Regt. Arenberg (Netherlands)

Title: Raised 1743 as the 2nd *Niederländisches National-Regiment* by Prince Arenberg; disbanded 1748.

Uniform: Red facings.

Regt. Göldlin

Titles: 1740 Göldlin, 1741 Kheul; disbanded 1747.

Uniform: Red facings.

Regt. Heister

Title: 1740 Heister; disbanded 1747

Uniform: Red facings.

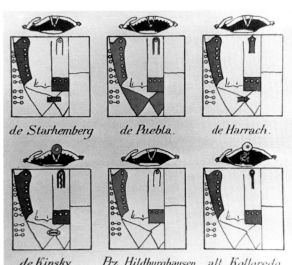

de Starhemberg   de Puebla   de Harrach

de Kinsky   Prz. Hildburghausen   alt Kolloredo

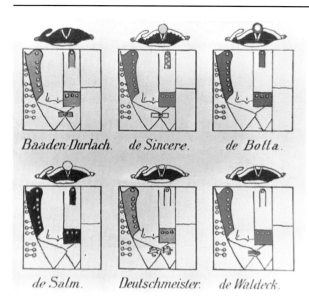

Infantry uniform, c. 1762; regiments numbered (top left to bottom right) 27, 54, 12, 14, 4 and 35; colour details in the text.

Regt. Marulli (Lombardy)

Title: 1740 Marulli; disbanded 1751

Uniform: Blue facings. The Gudenus MS of 1734 shows blue turnbacks, low cuffs revealing a vertical white flap, lapels (with buttons arranged one over two over three). waistcoat and breeches. The cartridge box bears a large brass Maltese cross, and small grenades in the lower corners; the grenadier cap has a blue ground, bearing a brass grenade, and a white or silver pointed upper edge with a central black line.

Regt. O'Gilvy (Bohemia)

Title: 1740 O'Gilvy; disbanded 1748.
Uniform: Blue facings.

Regt. Schmettau

Title: 1740 Schmettau. Disbanded 1741 when its *Inhaber*, Carl Christoph von Schmettau, deserted to Frederick the Great, in whose service he became a valued general, until he fell under something of a cloud following his surrender of Dresden.
Uniform: Red facings.

Regt. Sprecher

Title: Raised March 1743 in the Grisons (*Graubünden*), Habsburg possessions in eastern Switzerland; 1743 Sprecher von Bernegg (sometimes styled

Graubündtner-Regiment); disbanded 1749.
Uniform: Red facings.

Regt. Traun

Title: 1740 Traun; disbanded 1748.
Uniform: Red or blue facings.

Regt. Wallis

Titles: 1740 Wallis, 1746 Hagenbach; merged 1748 into Regt. Roth (no. 22), which then took the name Hagenbach.
Uniform: Rose-pink facings.

Stabs-Regiment

The *Stabs-Infanterie-Regiment* ('Staff Infantry') was formed for escort and headquarters duties in wartime (1758–63, 1778–79), and disbanded upon the conclusion of hostilities.
Uniform: Dark blue coat (without lapels) and waistcoat, red collar, cuffs and shoulder straps, white turnbacks with red oblong badges, yellow buttons arranged one over two over three (Ottenfeld indicates evenly-spaced), red pompon and rosettes; 'German' infantry legwear.

THE PLATES

A1: Grenadier, Regt. Los Rios (no. 9), c. 1748
This subject is typical of the style of grenadier uniform shown in the paintings of David Morier; in this case the cap has no ornaments other than the facing-coloured bag with yellow lace and tassel. The match case continued in use with grenadiers even after the hand grenade was no longer used; originally it held the smouldering slowmatch used to ignite the fuses of grenades. Note the white stockings worn under the gaiters.

A2: Grenadier, Regt. Waldeck (no. 35), c. 1748
Morier's paintings record many minor variations in grenadier uniform. In this case the cap bears an elaborate metal plate depicting a crowned shield backed by a trophy of arms, in addition to its facing-coloured bag; the facing colour is not displayed upon the lapels and lining; and the shoulder belt has a buckle and metal tip at the front.

A3: Oπ cer, Regt. Moltke (no. 13), c. 1750

Regt. Moltke had red facings in 1740, but light blue from 1743; yellow buttons, light blue or white shoulder strap, and red and yellow hat rosettes. This depicts the ordinary style of officers' uniform, with the partizan carried by most officers until 1759; field ranks carried weapons with more elaborate decoration and larger tassels.

B1: Feldwäbel, Regt. Thürheim (no. 25), c. 1757

Regt. Thürheim had red facings in 1740, blue 1742, and red 1748; yellow buttons, red shoulder strap (to which Ottenfeld indicates white piping) and red turnback badge (rectangular and dart-shaped are recorded, not indicated by Ottenfeld); red or red and yellow hat rosettes (Ottenfeld, red and white). This figure has typical NCO rank distinctions: metallic hat lace, cane, and the *Kurzgewehr*, for which a number of shapes of blade are recorded.

B2: Field oπ cer, Regt. Salm-Salm (no. 14), c. 1760

Regt. Salm-Salm had light blue facings in 1740, black 1748; yellow buttons, black or white shoulder strap, red and blue hat rosettes (Ottenfeld indicates white pompon and tassels). Morier shows a grenadier with black facings but white lapels and turnbacks, white buttons, and a red cap-bag with white lace and tassel. This officer wears the riding boots used by field officers for mounted service.

B3: Fusilier, Regt. Ligne (no. 38), c. 1759

Regt. Ligne wore rose-pink facings and oblong turnback badge (the family colour of de Ligne), white buttons, green hat rosettes; and, most unusually for Austrian uniforms, fringed rose-pink shoulder straps resembling epaulettes.

C1: Corporal, Regt. Harsch (no. 50), c. 1759

This shows the unique distinction of Regt. Harsch, as noted in the main text, of white tassel-ended lace loops. The *Kurzgewehr* illustrated has a spear blade of undulating sides, one of a number of recorded styles; another indication of rank is the cane, suspended in the usual manner from a lapel button.

C2: Fusilier, Regt. Deutschmeister (no. 4), c. 1760

Regt. Deutschmeister wore 'sapphire blue' facings (including waistcoat and turnbacks 1757), yellow buttons, white or blue shoulder strap, and the unique yellow fleur-de-lys turnback badge; yellow, or yellow and black hat rosettes. This man wears the infantry's full field equipment, and carries the 1754 musket.

C3: Fusilier, Regt. Wied (no. 28), c. 1760

Regt. Wied had green facings 1740, red 1743, green 1748; yellow buttons; shoulder strap green, or white with green edge and undulating line; scalloped hat lace, white pompon with green edge and red centre, yellow and black or yellow and green rosettes; an alternative pompon is recorded which substitutes yellow for white. Morier shows a grenadier with green facings and waistcoat, white turnbacks and buttons, and a brass grenade on the waist belt pouch.

D1: Private, Regt. Kökenyésdy de Vettes (no. 34), 1742

This figure, after Knötel, depicts the early Hungarian uniform, a development from 'national dress'

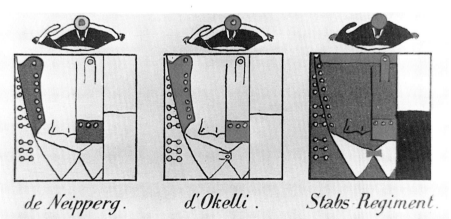

Infantry uniform, c. 1762; regiments numbered (left to right) 7, 45 and Stabs-Regiment; colour details in the text.

de Neipperg.   d'Okelli.   Stabs-Regiment.

with many features in common with hussar uniform, which evolved from the same origin. These included a braided jacket, barrelled sash, and tight pantaloons. The boots are the characteristic laced Hungarian pattern.

D2: Grenadier, Regt. Ujváryi (no. 2), c. 1748
This uniform, after Morier, represents the transition from Hungarian 'national dress' to a style more resembling that of the 'German' regiments, but retaining distinct Hungarian features in the legwear, braided waistcoat like a hussar dolman, barrelled sash, a coat with no lapels and lace loops fastening with toggles instead of buttons, and hussar-style waist belt. Morier shows a sabre of hussar style, apparently with separate waist belt for the bayonet. This is one of a number of recorded variations to the rule that the bags of grenadier caps were in the facing colour: Morier appears to depict a dark blue bag.

D3: Grenadier, Regt. Haller (no. 31), c. 1748
As shown in another of Morier's paintings, this uniform includes a number of interesting features, including the hussar-style leggings (*scharawaden*) worn over buff breeches. Note also the coat-loops in pairs, an exception to the later Hungarian style of six loops, one over two over three. The sabre is an old Hungarian type without a knuckle bow.

E1: Grenadier, Regt. Bethlén (no. 52), c. 1748
Another variation in Hungarian uniform is shown by

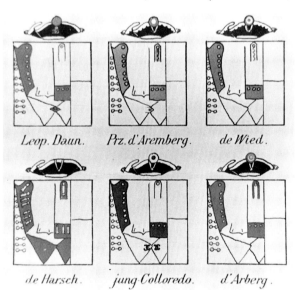

Leop. Daun. Prz. d'Aremberg. de Wied.

de Harsch. jung Colloredo. d'Arberg.

Morier for Regt. Bethlén, including unusual white pantaloons and a barrelled sash of a more elaborate design than usual. This unit is recorded as having red facings in 1743, blue in 1748, but green by 1757 (including waistcoat and turnbacks; the green must have been adopted much earlier to judge from Morier's painting), but light blue by 1762 (including waistcoat and breeches, but white turnbacks and shoulder straps), yellow buttons; white or blue tasselled lace on the coat, red on the waistcoat; red and yellow sash.

E2: Fusilier, Regt. Josef Esterházy (no. 37), 1762
This depicts the Hungarian uniform of the Seven Years' War period. Regt. Josef Esterházy wore red facings, shoulder strap, waistcoat, breeches and coat lace, red dart-shaped turnback badges edged white, green or blue lace on the waistcoat, white buttons, and a sash either green and red or white, or blue and red; yellow pompon with red centre, red and blue rosettes. This figure wears full equipment and carries the short sabre from a frog on the waist belt.

E3: Fusilier, Regt. Erzherzog Ferdinand (no. 2), 1762
Like Regt. Simbschèn (no. 53), Regt. Erzherzog Ferdinand (ex-Ujváryi, see Plate D2) was a Hungarian regiment which carried a sabretache, in this case blue with yellow scalloped edge and eagle device. Regimental distinctions included yellow facings (including pointed cuffs), lace and buttons, blue breeches and waistcoat, blue and yellow sash (Ottenfeld indicates yellow and white); yellow pompon, blue and yellow rosettes. This figure follows Knötel in depicting a short, hussar-style weapon suspended on slings.

F1: Officer, Regt. Toscana, c. 1758
The Tuscan Regiment, which joined the Austrian army by virtue of Maria Theresa's husband being duke of that state, was formed with an establishment of three battalions, each of six fusilier and two grenadier companies; one battalion was formed from each of the Tuscan army's three infantry regiments. All wore white with red facings (although a blue uniform

Infantry uniform, c. 1762; regiments numbered (top left to bottom right) 59, 21, 28, 50, 40 and 55; colour details in the text.

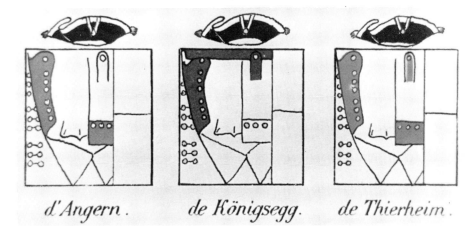

Infantry uniform, c. 1762; regiments numbered (left to right) 49, 16 and 25; colour details in the text.

d'Angern.   de Königsegg.   de Thierheim.

was adopted later), with white buttons for the 1st Regt. and yellow for the others, arranged evenly, in pairs and in threes for the 1st–3rd Regts. respectively. Officers' and NCOs' distinctions were like those of the Austrian army, in button-coloured lace; officers wore the Austrian sash. Grenadiers had fur caps with a brass grenade badge on the front, and a red bag; drummers wore yellow coats with black facings (the imperial colours) and silver lace.

F2: Officer, Regt. Gyulai (no. 51), c. 1762

This shows the Hungarian officers' uniform in the colouring of Regt. Gyulai; it includes characteristically Hungarian (or hussar-style) items in the hussar boots, barrelled sash in the colours of the *Feldbinde* of 'German' regiments, and a hussar-style sabre in place of the *épée* carried by 'German' officers.

F3: Fusilier, Regt. Gyulai (no. 51), c. 1762

Regt. Gyulai wore dark blue facings, shoulder strap, waistcoat and breeches, yellow buttons, red lace, blue and red sash, and turnback badge in the form of three white diamonds; white pompon with dark blue centre, and blue and white rosettes (yellow and black pompon and rosettes are also recorded).

F4: Fusilier, Regt. Haller (no. 31), c. 1762

This shows the development of Hungarian uniform from the style shown in Plate D3. Regt. Haller had light blue facings, waistcoat, breeches and lace (red lace on waistcoat), yellow buttons and red and blue sash. The sabre, as shown by Knötel, is of hussar style, suspended on slings, rather than the grenadier type carried on a frog.

G1: Hungarian grenadier

Plate G shows the infantry uniform introduced from 1767, including a single-breasted coat, a wider range of facing colours, and new headdress, in this case the restyled grenadier cap with embossed brass plate, a rear bag which no longer hung down, and a yellow pompon with black centre at the right. Distinctions for Hungarian regiments included pointed cuffs with a tasselled lace loop (styled *bärentatzen* or 'bear's paw'), and blue pantaloons with black and yellow braid.

G2: 'German' fusilier

The grey-brown greatcoat usually had the collar and shoulder strap piped in the facing colour; when not worn, it was carried rolled and folded on top of the knapsack, secured by white leather straps. This man wears the 1767 *Casquet* with its original decoration, a plate bearing the cyphers 'MT' and 'J', black and yellow pompon at the left, and scalloped lace edging. The fusilier sabre was suspended from the waist belt like grenadiers' sabres, but was most distinct from the absence of a knuckle bow.

G3: 'German' fusilier drummer

Drummers continued to wear ordinary uniform with the addition of wings, and lace on the facings, usually depicted with an undulating or crenellated edge. This figure follows Ottenfeld in showing the drum hoops in red and the facing colour, but recorded variations include hoops in the imperial yellow and black. The knapsack was normally carried over the right shoulder, hanging at the left hip (so as not to interfere with access to the cartridge box for men

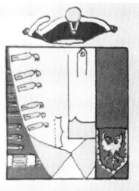
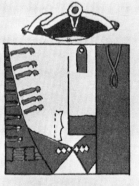

Erzh. Ferdinand.   Gyulai.   Preysach.

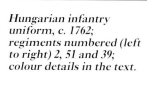

Hungarian infantry uniform, c. 1762; regiments numbered (left to right) 2, 51 and 39; colour details in the text.

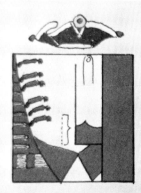
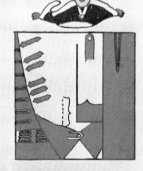
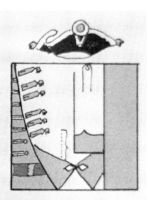

Nicol. Eszterházy. Josef Eszterházy   Forgách.

Hungarian infantry uniform, c. 1762; regiments numbered (left to right) 33, 37 and 32; colour details in the text.

armed with muskets), but for drummers the knap-sack was suspended over the left shoulder.

H1: Fusilier, Anhalt-Zerbst Battalion, 1761

Christian August, Furst of Anhalt-Zerbst, was a general in Prussian service who succeeded to the title in 1746 but died in 1747; his most famous offspring was Catherine the Great, Empress of Russia, but it was her brother Frederick Augustus who succeeded to Anhalt-Zerbst. He formed a battalion for imperial service, including 50 cavalrymen and a piece of artillery. The uniform illustrated is taken from a coloured copy of a contemporary print produced originally as an aid to recruiting; Knötel's version has a white musket sling and a yellow tip to the pompon. The same print shows grenadier uniform, like that of the fusilier but with a match case on the shoulder belt, and a fur grenadier cap with a brass grenade badge on the front and a red bag. Knötel's version shows a yellow sword knot with red fringe.

H2: Grenadier, Mainz Kreis-contingent, 1757

Although not officially part of the Austrian army, the *Reichsarmee* was formed to discharge the feudal responsibility of providing troops to support the empire in time of crisis; it was supposed to have a nucleus of Austrian troops, but sometimes only small numbers could be spared. *Reichsarmee* units wore uniforms styled on those of Austria or Prussia; the Mainz contingent, which fought at Rossbach, formed part of the contribution of the Rhenish *Kreis* (area), and was one of those which wore Austrian styles.

H3: Grenadier, Hessen-Darmstadt Kreis-contingent, 1757

The Hessen-Darmstadt *Kreis-Regiment* formed part of the contribution of the Upper Rhenish *Kreis* to the *Reichsarmee*, and unlike the majority which fought at Rossbach was an excellent corps which performed with distinction. It was one of the *Reichsarmee* units to wear Prussian-style uniform, including metal-fronted mitre cap; this illustration follows Knötel in depicting a brass cap plate, although a recorded alternative shows a white metal plate with coloured lion device, and 14 loops on the coat-breast. Although some of the states which contributed men to the *Reichsarmee* maintained their own army, it was usual for regiments to be formed specifically for *Reichsarmee* service, as in this case, rather than sending an existing regiment; in this sense, the *Reichsarmee* units were more 'imperial' (and by extension Austrian) than belonging to their own native states.

Bibliography

A number of important references were noted in MAA 271: *The Austrian Army 1740–80 I: Cavalry*, of which a number are listed below.

The most important work in English on the Austrian army of the mid-18th century is *The Army of Maria Theresa: The Armed Forces of Imperial Austria 1740–1780*, Christopher Duffy, Newton Abbot 1977 (latest edn. Doncaster 1990), which is essential reading and includes a comprehensive bibliography. *Die Österreichische Armee von 1700 bis 1867*, R. von Ottenfeld & O. Teuber, Vienna 1895, remains a significant reference to uniforms and equipment, as do the plates of Richard Knötel's *Uniformenkunde* series, and *Handbuch der Uniformkunde*, R. & H. Knötel and H. Sieg, Hamburg 1937, r/p 1964. An important reproduction of 1762 uniform illustra-

tions, the 'Albertina MS', is *Das Heer Maria Theresias: Faksimile-Ausgabe der Albertina-Handschrift 'Dessins des Uniformes des Troupes I.I. et R.R. de l'armée 1762'*, F. Kornauth, Vienna 1973. David Morier's paintings are illustrated in *Military Drawings & Paintings in the Royal Collection*, A.E. Haswell Miller & N.P. Dawnay, London 1966–70. Interesting early illustrations are reproduced in *Reiter, Husaren und Grenadiere: Die Uniformen der Kaiserlichen Armee am Rhein 1734: Zeichnungen des Philipp Franz, Freiherrn von Gudenus*, Dr. H. Bleckwenn, Dortmund 1979. *Austro-Hungarian Infantry 1740–1762* (Birmingham 1982) and *The Reichsarmee* (Birmingham 1983), both by R.D. Pengel & G.R. Hurt, are useful compilations. Details of the Tuscan Regiment may be found in an article, 'The "Reggimento di Toscana" in the Seven Years War', P. Crociani & M. Brandani, in the journal *Tradition*, no. 52; and in *Uniformi Militari Italiane del Settecento*, M. Brandani, P. Crociani & M. Fiorentino, Rome 1976. The general military costume of the period, including Austria, is covered excellently in *Uniforms of the Seven Years War*, J. Mollo, Poole 1977; and further material on the Austrian army of the later 18th century is contained in MAA 176, *Austrian Army of the Napoleonic Wars (1): Infantry*, London 1986. *Die Österreichische Armee im Siebenjährigen krieg*, L.-H. Thümmler, Berlin 1993, is a valuable reproduction of a contemporary manuscript.

Notes sur les planches en couleur

A1 Style d'uniforme typique des grenadiers inspiré des tableaux de David Morier. Cet exemple de calot ne comporte pas d'ornements sauf sur le sac. Remarquez les bas blancs portés sous les guêtres. A2 Variations régimentales typiques illustrées par Morier: plaque métallique de calot travaillée, absence de couleur de parement sur les revers et la doublure, bandoulière avec attaches métalliques à l'avant. A3 Les parements bleu ciel remplacèrent la rouge après 1743, Ce Style de pertuisane était porté par la plupart des jeunes officiers jusqu'à 1759.

B1 Dentelle métallique sur chapeau, bâton et hallebarde Kurzgewehr sont des distinctions typiques NCO. Ottenfeld montre un passepoil blanc sur la bandoulière rouge. Des badges de revers de forme rectangulaire et pointue sont mentionnés. B2 Morier peint un grenadier avec des parements noirs (1748–) mais des revers blancs. Les officiers de campagne portaient des bottes de cheval. B3 Cet uniforme est inhabituel par ses épaulettes àfranges roses, la couleur de parement de la famille De Ligne.

C1 Des boucles en dentelle blanche se terminant par des glands étaient la seule distinction du Regt. Harsch. Le Kurzgewehr était fabriqué avec différentes formes de lames. C2 Matériel de campagne typique. Notez le badge de revers unique de ce régiment en forme de fleur de lys. C3 Wied portait des parements rouges 1743–48 puis revint au vert. Les bandoulières auraient pu être vertes ou blanches avec un passepoil vert en zig-zag. Morier peint un grenadier portant une grenade en cuivre sur la bourse de ceinture, des parements et un gilet verts et des revers blancs.

D1 Figure selon Knötel illustrant un des premiers uniformes hongrois clairement inspiré du cosume national. Notez de nombreuses caractéristiques 'hussardes' et les bottines lacées hongroises caractéristiques. D2 D'après Morier – l'uniforme a évolué mais conserve les caractéristiques nationales. Remarquez le sac de calot bleu foncé, une des nombreuses variations tirées des couleurs des parements et le sabre et te sabretache de style husard. D3 D'après Morier: remarquez les culottes de style

Farbtafeln

A1 Typischer Uniformstil der Grenadiere, Gemälden von David Morier nachempfunden. Dieses Beispiel für die Mütze hat keine Verzierungen, außer auf dem Kopfteil. Man beachte die weißen Strümpfe, die unter den Gamaschen getragen wurden. A2 Typische Regimentsabweichungen nach Morier: kunstvolle Mützenplakette aus Metall, keine farbige Verblendung am Revers und Futter, Schultergurt mit Metallverschluß an der Vorderseite. A3 Die hellblaue Verblendung ersetzte nach 1743 die rote. Diese Art der Hellebarde wurde bis 1759 von den meisten rangniedrigen Offizieren getragen.

B1 Die metallisch glänzende Hutschnur, der Stock und die Streitwaffe *Kurzgewehr* sind die typischen Kennzeichen eines Unteroffiziers. Bei Ottenfeld sieht man weiße Paspeln an der roten Schulterklappe; rechteckige sowie pfeilförmige Aufschlagsabzeichen sind überliefert. B2 Bei Morier trägt der Grenadier schwarze (1748) Verblendung, aber weiße Revers und Aufschläge. Die Stabsoffiziere trugen Reitstiefel. B3 Das ungewöhnliche Merkmal dieser Uniform sind die befransten Epauletten in der rosa Verblendungsfarbe der Familie De Ligne.

C1 Das Regt. Harsch war durch weiße Litzenschlaufen, an denen Quastern angebracht waren, unverwechselbar gekennzeichnet. Das *Kurzgewehr* wurde mit unterschiedlichen Klingenformen gefertigt. C2 Hier ist die typische, komplette Feldausrüstung illustriert; man beachte das unverwechselbare Aufschlagsabzeichen mit der bourbonischen Lilie des Regiments. C3 *Wied* hatte 1743–48 rote Verblendung, danach kehrte man zur grünen Farbe zurück; die Schulterklappen waren vermutlich grün, oder aber weiß mit grünen Paspeln und einer Schlangenlinie. Morier zeigt einen Grenadier mit einer Messinggranate an der Gürteltasche, grüne Verblendung und Weste sowie weiße Aufschläge.

D1 Die Knötel nachempfundene Figur belegt deutliche, daß die frühe ungarische Uniform von der Landestracht abgeleitet ist; man beachte die vielen "husarenartigen" Merkmale und die charakteristischen ungarischen Schnürstiefel.

hussard, ou scharawaden, les boucles de manteau par paires et la forme ancienne du sabre hongrois.

E1 Morier peint un pantalon blanc inhabituel et une ceinture large sophistiquée. Quatre couleurs de parements sont enregistrées en 1743, 1748, 1757 et 1762. **E2** Style d'uniforme hongrois typique de la période de la Guerre de Sept Ans avec matériel de campagne. Remarquez le sabre orné de brandebourgs. **E3** Comme le sujet de **D2**, l'uniforme de cette unité de style hussard, allant même jusqu'au port du sabretache. Figure d'après Knötel.

F1 Cette unié se joignit à l'armé autrichienne lorsque le Duc de Toscane épousa Maria Theresa. Les trois bataillons portaient du blanc et des parements rouges mais différents boutons (blancs, espacements égaux; jaunes, en paires et en groupes de trois respectivement). Les officiers portaient des ceintures autrichiennes. **F2** Uniforme typique des officiers hongrois avec les distinctions de ce régiment **F3** Fusilier du même régiment avec parements bleu foncé, gilet et culottes; dentelle rouge, ceinture bleue et rouge et badge à triple diamant sur les revers. Notez les couleurs de l'unité dans le pompon du calot et dans les rosettes. **F4** Le développement de l'uniforme hongrois à partir de celui illustré à **D3**. Knötel montre cet arrangement du sabre, à la hussarde, pour le Regt. Haller.

G Cette planche illustre l'uniforme d'infanterie de 1767 avec un manteau à boutonnage simple, une gamme de couleurs de parements bien plus grande et de nouveaux couvre-chefs. **G1** le calot de grenadier redessiné portait une plaque de cuivre en relief et le sac arrière n'était plus pendant. Notez le pompon noir et jaune sur la droite. Les régiments hongrois avaient des manchettes pointues et une boucle de dentelle avec des glands (bärentatz') et un pantalon bleu avec des décorations en soutache noire et jaune. **G2** Le Casquet de 1767 dans sa forme originale. Le manteau gris/marron avait généralement un passepoil de la même couleur que les parements sur le col et sur la bandoulière. Le sabre des fusiliers n'avait pas de garde. **G3** Inspiré d'Ottenbfeld. Remarquez les 'nids d'hirondelles' àl'épaule, la dentelle spéciale et le havresac jeté sur l'épaule gauche plutôt que droite.

H1 Ce bataillon fut recruté pour servir avec les autrichiens par le frère de Catherine la Grande. Une copie en couleur d'un imprimé de recrutement contemporain a survécu. Knötel indique de petites variations. **H2** Ce contingent de Rhénanie du Reichsarmee se battit à Rossbach avec un uniforme de style autrichien. **H3** L'une des rares unités Reichsarmee de bonne qualité. Ce contingent portait un uniforme de style prussien.

D2 Nach Morier – die Uniform bildet sich heraus, doch werden einige Merkmale der Landestracht beibehalten. Man beachte das dunkelblaue Kopfteil der Mütze, eine mehrerer Abweichungen von den Verblendungsfarben und die Säbeltasche im Husarenstil. **D3** Nach Morier: man beachte die husarenartigen Hosen bzw. *Scharawaden*: die paarweisen Jackenschlaufen und die alte ungarische Säbelform.

E1 Morier zeigt ungewöhnliche, weiße Plunderhosen und eine kunstvolle Laufschärpe. 1743, 1748, 1757 und 1762 sind vier verschiedene Verblendungsfarben überliefert. **E2** Typisch ungarischer Uniformstil aus der Zeit des Siebenjährigen Krieges mit kompletter Feldausrüstung; man beachte den Säbel an der Gürtelschlaufe. **E3** Wie bei **D2** trägt auch diese Einheit den Husarenstil bis hin zur *Sabretache*. Darstellung nach Knötel.

F1 Diese Einheit stieß zur österreichischen Armee, da der Herzog von Toskana Maria Theresia heiratete; die drei Bataillone trugen weiß, rot verblendet, hatten jedoch unterschiedliche knöpfe (weiß, gleichmäßig angeordnet; gelb, paarweise beziehungsweise in Dreiergruppen). Die Offiziere trugen österreichische Schärpen. **F2** Typisch ungarische Offiziersuniform mit den Kennzeichen dieses Regiments. **F3** Füsilier des gleichen Regiments mit dunkelblauer Verblendung. Weste und Kniehosen; rote Litze; blaue und rote Schärpe; und dreifaches Rhombenabzeichen auf den Aufschlägen. Man beachte die Farben der Einheit an Pompon und den Rosetten. **F4** Die Entwicklung der ungarischen Uniform aus der Abbildung **D3**. Bei Knötel sieht man den husarenartigen Säbel, der wie beim Regt Haller getragen wird.

G Diese Farbtafel zeigt die Infanterieuniform des Jahres 1767 mit der einreihigen Jacke, einer großen Farbskala bei der Verblendung und neuer Kopfbedeckung. **G1** Die Grenadiermütze in der neuen Form hatte eine geprägte Messingplakette und das hintere Kipfteil hing nicht mehr herunter; man beachte den schwarz gelben Pompon auf der rechten Seite. Die ungarischen Regimenter hatten schwarz zulaufende Manschetten mit einer Schnurschlaufe mit Quaste (*Bärentatze*) sowie blaue Pluderhosen mit schwarz-gelber Litzenverzierung. **G2** Der *Casquet* de Jahres 1767 in der ursprünglichen Form. Der graubraune Überzieher hatte normalerweise Paspeln in der Verblendungsfarbe am Kragen und an den Schulterklappen. Der Säbel der Füsiliere hatte keinen Schutzbogen. **G3** Nach Ottenfeld; man beachte die "Schwalbennester" an den Schultern, besonders Schnur und den Tornister, der über die linke anstelle der rechten Schulter gehängt wurde.

H1 Dieses Bataillon wurde vom Bruder von Katharina der Großen für den Wehrdienst in der österreichischen Armee zusammengestellt. Eine farbige Kopie eines zeitgenössischen Anwerbedrucks ist überliefert; bei Knötel zeigen sich leichte Abweichungen. **H2** Dieses Rheinland-Kontingent der *Reichsarmee* kämpfte bei Rossbach und trug Uniformen österreichischer Machart. **H3** Dieses Kontingent ist eine der wenigen hochwertigen Einheiten der *Reichsarmee* und trug Uniformen im preußischen Stil.